FRESHFIELDS

MANAGEMENT CONTRACTING
LAW & PRACTICE

Cavendish
Publishing
Limited

FRESHFIELDS

MANAGEMENT CONTRACTING
LAW & PRACTICE

Written by
Members of Freshfields'
Construction and Engineering Group

Cavendish
Publishing
Limited

First published in Great Britain 1994 by Cavendish Publishing Limited,
The Glass House, Wharton Street, London WC1X 9PX
Telephone: 071-278 8000   Facsimile: 071-278 8080

This book states the law and practice as at 1 December 1993. It is not
intended to be a comprehensive study, nor to provide legal advice, and
should not be treated as a substitute for specific advice concerning
individual situations.

A CIP catalogue record for this book is available from the British Library.

ISBN 1-874241-18-X

Printed and bound in Great Britain

PREFACE

I would like to thank all the members of Freshfields'
Construction and Engineering Group who contributed to this
book, particularly Sarah Parry who edited it for us. We are also
grateful to Butterworth & Co (Publishers) Ltd for permitting us to
use here (in Chapter 2) our discussion of different contracting
methods first published in Emden's *Construction Law* (1993).

Sally Roe

CONTENTS

CONTENTS

CONTENTS

CONTENTS

CONTENTS

CONTENTS

TABLE OF STATUTES

TABLE OF CASES

TABLE OF JCT 87 DOCUMENTATION

JCT Management Contract

Articles of Agreement

Conditions (clauses)

Appendices

Schedules

JCT Works Contract/1

JCT Works Contract/2

Conditions (clauses)

JCT Works Contract/3

Practice Notes

CHAPTER 1

OVERVIEW

This book addresses a variety of issues arising from the method of construction procurement known as management contracting. By way of introduction, Chapter 2 contains a general description and comparison of the range of construction procurement methods. This briefly summarises key features of the management contract and sets it in context; points made in the introductory chapter are expanded in the body of the book.

Why should management contracting be treated differently? Like other methods of contracting for the construction of a building, it creates relationships and associated rights and obligations between the parties involved which are different from those arising under what is now thought of as the 'traditional' main contractor type of building contract.

What sets management contracting apart is perhaps that, while it deals with the parties' rights and obligations in a way wholly distinct from that of a traditional system, it retains a superficial similarity to the traditional structure. This similarity can be deceptive. For this reason if no other, features peculiar to management contracting may be said to merit separate treatment.

This book aims to cover the spectrum of issues which arise in relation to most types of construction contract, picking out aspects apparently peculiar to management contracts.

Until 1987 there was no published standard form of management contract in the UK. Instead, a number of tailor-made or bespoke forms of contract had come into use, developed mainly by major contracting organisations. In 1987 the Joint Contracts Tribunal finally agreed and published its long-awaited standard form of management contract with associated works contract documentation. The JCT 87 documentation consists of a management contract ('the JCT Management Contract'), a works contract (JCT Works Contract/1 contains the invitation to tender, tender and articles of agreement and JCT Works Contract/2 contains the works contract conditions), and an employer/works contractor direct agreement (JCT Works Contract/3). This set of standard forms has been widely used. However, it seems sometimes to be used in a highly customised and amended way and has not entirely replaced bespoke forms.

This book is not intended to be a specific commentary on or annotation of the JCT 87 documentation. However, the JCT 87 forms are referred to, where appropriate, as providing a norm for clauses dealing with particular aspects of management contracting. (Also, some topics can only be illustrated satisfactorily by reference to the published JCT 87 forms because of constraints on quoting bespoke forms.)

Although management contracting has been in use for some time, the effects and consequences of the relationships, rights and obligations of the parties have not yet been thoroughly explored in court. Where possible, the authors have drawn analogies with principles from case law in other areas.

CHAPTER 2

DIFFERENT CONTRACTING METHODS

Procuring the construction of a building or engineering work is usually a lengthy operation involving many variable factors. These include:

- the balance between the anticipated cost, the time allowed and the quality of work required;
- the nature of the site and the availability of access to it;
- the availability of professional skills;
- the availability of a completed design;
- the availability of materials; and
- the extent of the employer's own management resources.

Like the terms of any commercial contract, the structure and conditions of a construction contract may be freely negotiated and agreed to take account of these matters. They are subject only to such generally applicable constraints as the Unfair Contract Terms Act 1977. However, several distinct methods of contracting have evolved, dividing the risks and responsibilities of construction between employers and contractors in a variety of ways.

The methods differ in two main areas: the basis on which the contractor's work is to be priced and paid for, and the degree or nature of responsibility given to the contractor for management and design.

1 DIFFERENT BASES FOR PRICING AND PAYMENT

Lump sum or fixed price

A building contract priced in the traditional way requires the contractor to carry out and complete specified work for a fixed sum agreed in advance. Under this system, the design needs to be virtually complete and the work quantified when it is put out to tender. Contractors must be able to price the project accurately when tendering.

To ensure uniformity and accuracy in the description of work given to contractors, bills of quantities will be drawn up according to a published standard method of measurement. If any item of work or activity covered by the standard method is omitted from the bills but subsequently needs to be carried out, the contractor will be entitled to an addition to the original contract price. (An example might be unpriced excavation in rock, as in *C Bryant & Son v Birmingham Hospital Saturday Fund* (1938)).

A lump sum contract will frequently, though not necessarily, be an 'entire' contract. In such cases, the price is stated to be for completion of the whole of the work and the contractor's right to payment depends on his complete performance of that work (eg *Appleby v Myers* (1867) and see also *Tern Construction Group Ltd (In Administrative Receivership) v RBS Garages Ltd* (1993)). However, this will be subject in appropriate cases to the principle of substantial performance or the possibility of recovery on a quantum meruit.

In practice, an employer who has signed a 'fixed price' contract will usually end up paying more than the original lump sum. This tends to happen even where the bills of quantity are accurate. However, there are usually only a few contractually binding reasons for making additions or adjustments to the lump sum. These include the following.

Variations

If the employer or his professional team has a change of mind or is obliged to alter the requirements for the work, the adjustment may entitle the contractor to extra money.

Contractor's direct losses and expenses

Construction contracts often entitle the contractor to reimbursement for any direct loss and expense he suffers if the progress of the work is delayed for certain specified reasons. These may include events over which neither the contractor nor the employer has control. The employer needs to bear the risk for such events, if he wishes to avoid the contractor including them in his price at the outset. But the contractor may also be entitled to reimbursement if delays are caused by matters wholly within the control of the employer or his professional team.

Fluctuations

Some of the quoted rates and prices on the basis of which a contractor calculates a lump sum may be adjustable to reflect inflation over the contract period. Index-linking may take account of fluctuating tax rates and levels of national insurance contribution, as well as changes in the costs of labour, materials and so on. A contract where the fixed price cannot be adjusted according to final details of supply or specification but which is adjustable to reflect fluctuations is sometimes referred to as a 'firm' price contract rather than a true fixed price contract.

Despite all these potential variables, the essence of a lump sum contract is that in principle it provides a set price for a given amount of work within a given timescale, with price, work and timescale being quantified at the outset.

Remeasurement

Instead of a lump sum calculated on previously measured quantities, a contract may provide for payment for completed work which is measured as it proceeds.

Under this system, the contractor is paid for all the work properly done in performing the contract, whether or not the work was anticipated at the outset.

Remeasurement contracts are used where work cannot be fully quantified at the tendering stage. This may be because the design drawings from which bills of quantities are drawn up are only in preliminary form or incomplete. Or it may be because the project is bound to require a significant amount of unforeseen or unquantifiable work - something common in civil engineering contracts, where the degree of below-ground work involved usually makes it impracticable to assess detailed quantities in advance. Estimated or approximate bills of quantities may still be used for tendering, to allow comparison of tenders.

Certain works which are not quantifiable at the outset may be carried out on a remeasurement basis, while other works which can be quantified may be let on a lump sum basis.

The contract price in remeasurement contracts is sometimes referred to as the 'ascertained final sum'. This is a moving figure which changes in line with what has been completed and measured, calculated according to tendered unit rates. The eventual contract price is the total of all the payments certified from time to time during the progress of the work. But even this moving target may be subject to all the variables that can operate on lump sum prices, such as fluctuations, claims for loss and expense caused by specified events, and variations to the work (as distinct from additional measured work).

Cost reimbursement or cost plus fee

This method of procurement may be thought of as being at the opposite end of the spectrum from lump sum or fixed price contracts.

Here the employer pays the contractor the actual cost incurred in carrying out or procuring the works plus a fee or element of profit for the contractor, which is usually calculated as a percentage of the cost of the works. The actual cost of the works is often called the 'prime cost'.

In any cost reimbursement contract it needs to be made clear at the outset what items of the contractor's own organisation costs are admissible as prime costs and what items the employer expects to be absorbed within the fee. Some of the costs of the work which are of an organisational nature may be agreed as a lump sum separate from the fee and prime cost.

Cost reimbursement contracts have frequently been used in government contracting, for supply as well as works contracts. They have been particularly common in projects involving a significant amount of long term research and development work. The Joint Contracts Tribunal published a standard form of cost plus fee contract in 1967, but the system seems not to have been widely used until the advent of management contracting systems.

The employer only pays for the labour, plant and materials actually used. The employer therefore receives the benefit of any savings made by the management contractor, but also bears the cost of overcoming errors, omissions and design changes. The problem with cost reimbursement contracts is that the employer must ensure that each item of work is carried out efficiently and economically. The incentive that a contractor has in a fixed price contract to purchase the cheapest materials, employ the most economical labour and use the most cost-effective plant and construction methods is not present. These drawbacks can, however, be minimised by use of a target cost.

There are various means of calculating the contractor's reward or fee element. Common examples are costs plus fixed fee, costs plus fluctuating fee, and target cost.

Costs plus fixed fee

The fee is fixed as a lump sum or percentage rate by reference to the estimated overall cost of the works. A drawback may be that a fee calculated as a percentage of actual costs may minimise a contractor's incentive to control costs.

Costs plus fluctuating fee

An initial lump sum or percentage fee can be adjusted in line with significant increases or decreases in the actual cost of the works. This may be done either as a linear progression or by reference to a threshold (or series of thresholds) in actual as compared with budgeted cost. Again, a fee rising on simple incremental terms may not give much incentive for cost control.

Target cost

To provide the incentive for a tight control of costs, the contractor's fee may be varied in inverse proportion to the difference between the actual final cost of the work and the initial budgeted 'target' cost. A target cost or cost plan is agreed as an estimate for the works. This figure can be adjusted while the work is in progress to take account of factors such as variations or interference with the works by the employer. When the work is finished, the target cost (adjusted if necessary) is compared with the actual final cost. The original fee, whether fixed or percentage, can then be varied according to a predetermined formula. The formula can be designed to allow the contractor a greater or lesser share in the benefit of any savings which have been made.

Guaranteed maximum price

This may be thought of as a particular type of cost reimbursement contract. In addition to providing a mechanism for controlling the level of the contractor's fee, the contract imposes a ceiling on the amount of prime cost the employer will pay for the works as a whole.

Such a ceiling may provide an alternative means of spreading the risk for cost overruns between the employer and the contractor. In agreeing to a maximum price, the contractor takes on the risk of inaccurately estimated prices for sub-contract packages tendered later. However, guaranteed maximum price structures may be altered by allowing changes in the ceiling to cover factors for which it is agreed that the contractor should not bear the risk.

2 DIFFERENT BASES FOR DESIGN OR MANAGEMENT RESPONSIBILITY

Traditional method

The traditional method is sometimes known as the 'employer-designed' method. Its essence is that the employer procures the design of his project independently of its construction. This has been the 'traditional' method of contracting since the late nineteenth century. It was perpetuated through the JCT 63 form (still widely used) and survives in the JCT 80 standard form and its variants for intermediate and minor works. It is also the basis of the major civil engineering forms of contract.

Under the traditional method, the employer engages an architect or engineer (and other consultants where necessary) to design the works. The completed or nearly-completed design can then be expressed in bills of quantities by the employer's quantity surveyor. The design and the bills then form the basis on which tenders are invited for the construction of the works. The selected main contractor undertakes full responsibility for the construction of the works. However, the design is the employer's responsibility, having already been undertaken by his professional team.

The main contractor may sub-contract some or all of the work to sub-contractors 'nominated' in advance by the employer through his professional team, or to 'domestic' sub-contractors selected by the main contractor himself. It should be borne in mind that by nominating sub-contractors under the JCT 80 form the employer relieves the main contractor of certain responsibility for the performance of the nominated sub-contractor. Even though the main contractor undertakes no design responsibility, nominated (and, increasingly, domestic) sub-contractors are likely to do so. Sub-contractors' design responsibilities need to be covered by separate direct agreements between the sub-contractors and the employer.

In theory, the traditional method is the most reliable way of establishing the eventual cost of a project before construction begins. It normally uses a lump sum or remeasurement pricing basis. Because the design is complete (or nearly complete) before tenders are made, it should be possible to obtain a fixed estimate of overall costs. That estimate should not need adjusting, except to reflect changes in the scope of the work resulting from changes to the design or from unforeseen circumstances. Changes in design will only be necessary if the employer later alters the definition of what is required.

As regards timing, under the traditional method the design must be complete before tenders can be invited and construction can begin. The trade-off for the (theoretical) certainty in the lump sum is the longer time needed for the project as a whole.

As regards quality, splitting responsibility for design and construction leaves room for dispute, if there is a problem, over whether the fault is one of design, or of construction, or of a mixture of the two. There is also the potential for conflict in sorting out whether an apparent design problem falls within the remit of the professional team or of sub-contractors carrying out specialist design.

The scope for such disputes, coupled with the extended timescale and the difficulty of making theoretical price certainty work out in practice, have contributed to the evolution of several other contracting methods.

Design and build

When the design and build method is used, the employer engages a single organisation to take responsibility for all aspects of the project, including both design and construction (which may then be sub-contracted). This arrangement leaves the employer with a single principal source of remedy for any problems, whether they involve design or construction. However, it is common for the employer to enter into additional direct agreements with sub-consultants and sub-contractors.

The design and build method may be considered suitable because it is thought that the contractor alone possesses the specialist knowledge and skill to design and carry out specialist works or, in other cases, that there will be a saving of costs or time or both compared with the traditional method.

Design and build contracts are sometimes referred to as 'package deal' contracts or, particularly in civil engineering or mechanical and electrical plant work, as 'turnkey' contracts. This sums up the idea of an employer obtaining the complete design and construction of a plant which, once completed, needs only the turn of a key to make it work.

A design and build contractor will often seek to restrict his responsibilities for design to the normal standard of professional liability, namely to use the reasonable care and skill of an averagely-competent member of the profession. (This occurs, for example, in the JCT 81 standard form With Contractor's Design.) A contractor liable to any greater extent may find that design sub-consultants are reluctant to take on the same degree of responsibility, because their professional indemnity insurance may not cover liability greater than the normal professional standard.

In all design and build systems, someone in the employer's organisation must draw up an outline requirement as the basis on which the design and construction are to be carried out. This brief is commonly referred to as the 'employer's requirements'. The employer may use a project manager or even engage his own professional team to help draw up the brief, which will later be handed on to the contractor and his professional team. This, of course, means that the employer and his team remain responsible for design contained in the brief so that, although design and build is perceived as placing responsibility for design and construction with the contractor, some residual responsibility remains with the employer and his team. Sometimes the employer's team will later be taken on as sub-consultants to the design and build contractor.

It has been said that employers using the design and build system may miss out on the degree of independent professional advice available under traditional contracting methods, because the contractor engages the professional team. An employer with no project management resources of his own may therefore have additional reason to engage an outside project or design manager to help oversee the design and build contractor and probably also to help define the employer's requirements.

Design and build contracts are normally priced on a lump sum basis. As usual, the lump sum can be adjusted to reflect variations in the employer's requirements. It is sometimes thought that the contractor's relative freedom within the bounds of the employer's requirements may operate against the employer. This freedom is said to enable contractors to minimise cost by reducing the quality of the detailed design specification, for example in the area of building finishes. Whether or not this is true, design and build contracts generally place a relatively high level of risk and responsibility on contractors, and employers may expect to find this reflected in prices.

Management contracting

Management contracting is a derivative of the traditional method. The 'management contractor' occupies the position held by the main contractor under the traditional method. The employer still engages his own professional team to undertake the design. Like a traditional contractor, a management contractor engages a number of sub-contractors who actually carry out the construction work. The management contractor's role is effectively confined to managing and co-ordinating the performance of his various sub-contractors, who are usually referred to as 'works contractors'.

The management contractor does no actual construction work himself but exercises co-ordination, time, costs and quality control over the works contractors and provides site facilities for their common use. The management contractor is generally engaged before the design is completed so that he can work with the professional team and exercise some influence over the preparation of the design. An experienced management contractor will be able to comment on the 'buildability' of the design and will be principally responsible for planning and programming the sequence of the works.

The main difference of substance between a management contract and a traditional one is that the management contractor does not bear ultimate responsibility for the performance of the works contractors. The management contractor is normally protected by a clause in the contract which makes his liability to the employer no greater than whatever he can recover from defaulting works contractors.

This system is designed to place a much lower degree of risk on the shoulders of the management contractor than a traditional contract would place on the main contractor. The management contractor's reward is therefore usually expressed as a fee, calculated by a formula based on the actual cost of the works. In addition to this of course, the employer pays for the cost of the works, on a 'prime cost' basis. A management contract is thus a cost reimbursement contract rather than a lump sum one.

Management contracting developed mainly for use on 'fast track' projects where, because of an urgent need to complete (usually due to financial pressures on the employer), construction has to begin before the design is finished. In this situation a contractor cannot quote a fixed price at the start of the job. It follows that a method based on cost reimbursement plus fee is more appropriate.

Because the risk to the contractor under this system is low, his fee is likely to be less than his margin on sub-contractors' prices under a traditional main contract, where he would take the risk of their prices as part of a lump sum. Another intended advantage of the system for the employer is that it enables the management contractor to act in effect as a member of the employer's professional team. The contractor's fee should not increase through his own administration of the prime cost of the work (other than under target cost systems) and he will not himself be able to claim the extra costs (such as costs for delay) that he would if he were a main contractor. He ought therefore to have more incentive to act in the employer's best interests, like the rest of the employer's professional team. This is a step away from the position of a traditional main contractor, whose relationship with his employer is frequently seen as adversarial.

However, management contracting is also thought to have disadvantages for the employer. These include various technical legal difficulties in pursuing any claims that might arise against the management contractor and works contractors. The method may also be more expensive than the traditional method. Employers have to set these potential problems against the time saved through using management contracts.

Construction management

Construction management has developed as a variant of management contracting, and takes it to its logical conclusion. However, when used for a completed or almost fully-completed design, it may be viewed as an extension of traditional contracting that uses the services of several main contractors rather than one.

To the extent that it derives from management contracting, construction management recognises that the management contractor is not in principle responsible to the employer for the performance of works contractors. Construction management therefore takes the construction manager out of the works contract chain altogether. It treats him as just another consultant directly engaged by the employer. The employer himself directly employs all the trades that would have been sub-contractors to the main contractor under the traditional method. They become, in effect, a collection of parallel main contractors to the employer. Under this system they are generally referred to as 'trade contractors'.

For construction management to work, the employer needs to be able to cope with the direct administration of a large number of trade contractors. The construction manager's role is to assist the employer in this, managing and co-ordinating the work packages of each trade contractor to produce an organised whole. The construction manager's responsibility, like that of the rest of the professional team, is limited to the exercise of reasonable skill and care in the performance of his duties. He will not normally carry any responsibility for the actual performance of trade contractors, a risk which is instead taken by the employer.

Construction management is sometimes considered to be suitable only for more experienced employers with a substantial continuing requirement for construction procurement. Such employers are more likely to have the internal resources necessary to run such an administratively complex system.

Conclusion

This chapter is only an overview of the principal methods of contracting used in building and engineering projects. Variants abound. In many cases the contractor will accept greater responsibility for elements of the design of the project. For example, just as the design and build method evolved as a variant of the traditional method of contracting, so it is not uncommon for a design and management contracting method to be used as a version of management contracting. Under such a system, the management contractor takes responsibility for the design of the project and then engages his in-house design team or independent consultants to perform the actual design work.

The need to choose the right method and select or draft the right form of contract gives rise to difficult decisions. These decisions always involve, in some way, the division of risk between employer, contractor and other parties. It is often said, with reason, that the calibre and attitudes of the people involved in a project will ensure its success (or failure), whatever method or form of contract is used. But a suitable method of contracting, efficiently implemented, will always be a considerable help, given the near-inevitability in construction projects of something unforeseen causing specifications, budgets and programmes to change.

CHAPTER 3

BACKGROUND

1 DEVELOPMENT OF MANAGEMENT CONTRACTING

In Chapter 2, we described the traditional kind of construction contract. Numerous variants of this system have developed. They allow more or less of the detailed design work to be the responsibility of the main contractor; more or less of the contract price to be denominated at actual or 'prime' cost with contractor's fees applied to it at an agreed rate; and more or less measurement or remeasurement of completed work as the benchmark for valuation and payment.

However, in virtually all variants of the traditional system, the main contractor is responsible for building a structure to the given design (or engaging sub-contractors to build it). He takes full responsibility for workmanship, materials and compliance with specifications. In return, he receives the agreed 'contract' sum (or 'ascertained final sum' or 'prime cost plus fee') which may have been modified to reflect variations in the scope of the work, claims for loss or expense caused by delay or disruption in the progress of the works, or fluctuations in the cost of labour and materials or taxes.

Management contracting

Opinions differ as to just when management contracting emerged from this background as a distinct system of procuring construction. Forms of cost reimbursable contract, with the contractor being paid some sort of management fee related to the cost of the project, were used in the 1920s. Construction management arrangements have been used in the United States of America for decades and are generally considered to have been the forerunners of modern management contracting techniques and practices in the UK.

A number of features later seen as peculiar to management contracting have in fact been prevalent under traditional contracting systems for a considerable time. These are discussed in more detail in Chapter 4, but they include:

- the need for the main contractor to manage the activities of a number of sub-contractors;

- the tendency for the main contractor to undertake less and less direct construction work himself and let more and more of it in the sub-contract packages;
- the tendency of the architect or engineer to leave elements of the design, sometimes substantial, unfinished until after the commencement of construction, whether because of time constraints or because the employer has not yet been able to determine his own requirements;
- the use of numerous varieties of cost reimbursable contracts based on payment of prime cost plus a fee and subject to extensive cost monitoring procedures (particularly in the public sector); and
- the appointment, on a professional basis, of project managers experienced in construction as well as management techniques, to assist in looking after the employer's interests.

Although these features existed earlier, management contracting, as a distinct system of building procurement in reasonably widespread use in the UK, probably emerged in the 1970s and took flight in the early 1980s when the JCT began preparations for a standard form to deal with the 'new' system.

The development of management contracting as a distinct procurement system was primarily the result of growing dissatisfaction with a number of particular aspects of the traditional system of building procurement. These include the following in particular:

- the time taken to prepare a full design on the basis of which full bills of quantities could be drawn up, and the high cost of that time in terms of postponement of use or return;
- the almost habitually (it has been alleged) late completion of design by the professional team, or at least progressively late provision of certain elements of design information, resulting in increased scope for claims for delay and disruption from contractors and sub-contractors;
- lack of contractor involvement in the design process, resulting, it has been said, in designs that were less practical and less efficient and therefore took more time and cost more to build;
- proliferation of claims both for delay and disruption and for alleged variations, because of a desire to circumvent the commercial constraints imposed on contractors by lump sum pricing; the so-called fixed price contract seldom ended up as anything of the sort; and
- the tendency of the traditional structure to breed an 'adversarial' relationship between employer and main contractor and also between main contractor and professional team, resulting in the

main contractor devoting more time and resources to protecting his own commercial position than advancing the interests of the project.

An employer's three main goals are usually to achieve the optimum time, cost and quality for a building project. Partly because of the difficulties already mentioned, there arose a certain lack of confidence in the ability of traditional construction systems to achieve the goals of time and cost, and there were often significant overruns on both. It is likely that the novel features which now characterise management contracting therefore developed as trends in methods of operating within the confines of the traditional system.

Particularly important in this context have been:

- the growing desire, or need, to overlap commencement of construction with the continuation of the detailed design process (the distinguishing feature of 'fast tracking' as it has become known);

- the adaptation of pricing methods based on cost plus fee rather than lump sum subject to variations; and

- professional management assistance in the construction process.

As these trends have become more pronounced, so the management contract has emerged as a distinct system of building procurement.

2 RELATIONSHIP OF MAIN CONTRACTORS AND SUB-CONTRACTORS

A distinctive feature of management contracting is the main contractor's relationship with the employer as regards the sub-contractors.

A contracting party can often sub-contract performance to someone else so as to bind the other party to the main contract, provided the latter receives due performance. However, as a general rule, the primary contracting party will remain liable for breach of the main contract even if this is caused by a sub-contractor's breach of his sub-contract. The other party to the main contract will not be forced to rely on a remedy against the sub-contractor for breach. For example, a car repairer remains responsible to its customer for the proper carrying out of repairs to his car, even if some particular part of the work is entrusted (with the customer's agreement) to another specialist firm (*Stewart v Reavell's Garage* (1952)).

Standard forms of building contract under conventional methods take as read the principle that the main contractor is liable for his sub-contractor's performance. This usually has the result that no explicit provision is made for the main contractor's liability for sub-contractors' work. Instead, the forms tend to concentrate on defining the circumstances in which the contractor may or may not sub-contract part of the work.

Exceptions to main contractor's liability for sub-contractor's performance

There are some exceptions to this general principle, both implied by law and introduced by the terms of the contract itself.

Exceptions implied by law generally involve situations where the employer's normal reliance on the main contractor has in some way been transferred to the sub-contractor. This may be as a result of the nomination of a sub-contractor, or may arise simply from the circumstances surrounding the commissioning of work from the sub-contractor. For instance, in *University of Warwick v Sir Robert McAlpine* (1988), a type of epoxy resin was injected to remedy problems arising with ceramic wall tile cladding. The resin itself then caused the cladding to crack further. The architects recommended the resin and selected the sub-contractor who injected it; the main contractor was not involved in the decision to use it and expressed reservations about its suitability. It was held that the employer, through his architects, had relied on the skill and judgment of the selected sub-contractor rather than that of the main contractor. Accordingly, no warranty concerning the fitness of the resin could be implied into the main contract.

Exceptions may arise from the contract itself, either by implication or inference or by an express term. Exceptions created by implication or inference may arise when the contract provides specific consequences for a sub-contractor's breach which may be taken to exclude a more general liability for the breach (*John Jarvis Ltd v Rockdale Housing Association Ltd* (1987)). Alternatively, certain kinds of default by a nominated sub-contractor may be attributed to the employer rather than the main contractor, as in the *Bickerton, Percy Bilton* and *Fairclough Building* series of cases (*North West Metropolitan Hospital Board v TA Bickerton & Son Ltd* (1970); *Percy Bilton Ltd v Greater London Council* (1982); *Fairclough Building Ltd v Rhuddlan Borough Council* (1985)).

Express contractual provisions

The greatest scope for exception to the general principle is where that exception is expressly stated in the terms of the contract. Here the parties have the opportunity to define precisely the liabilities arising from their relationship. There are terms whose whole purpose is to exclude or modify the general rule.

Under traditional main contract systems, these provisions arise only in relation to aspects of liability for nominated sub-contractors. Clause 35.21 of JCT 80, for example, provides that the contractor is not responsible to the employer for any aspect of a nominated sub-contractor's work which is dealt with in the direct employer/nominated sub-contractor agreement, whether or not such an agreement has in fact been entered into. This covers design, selection of materials and satisfaction of performance specification. According to Clause 27(e) of JCT 63, final payment to a nominated sub-contractor releases the main contractor from liability (except for latent defects) for work, materials or goods executed or supplied by the sub-contractor under the sub-contract. This has been held to amount to an exemption clause relieving the contractor from liability in respect of the sub-contractor's failures (*Victoria University of Manchester v H Wilson* (1985)).

The peculiarity of the management contracting system, at least as it is generally understood, is that it creates an entirely distinct class of contract, an integral feature of which is commonly the inclusion of some express limitation of the management contractor's liability for his sub-contracted works contractors. However, rather than simply excluding that liability in certain circumstances, management contracts usually seek to achieve their purpose by limiting the management contractor's liability to the employer to the same level as the works contractor's liability to the management contractor. This peculiar, and in many cases central, aspect of the management contract is discussed in more detail in Chapter 11.

CHAPTER 4

THE NATURE OF
MANAGEMENT CONTRACTS

1 PRINCIPAL FEATURES

Management contracting developed as a distinct procurement system over a period of time and for a number of different, sometimes conflicting, reasons. Because the system developed through the use of many different types of bespoke contract without the assistance of a standard form, and has continued to do so even since the publication of the JCT 87 form, numerous varieties have evolved.

It is therefore not possible to describe the features of a classic management contract with pinpoint accuracy. Indeed, the latest published form of management contract - one of the 'options' included within the first edition of the New Engineering Contract published by the ICE in 1993 - is at variance with the JCT 87 form, even in the critical area of its treatment of the management contractor's liability for sub-contractors (Clause 26.1).

Certain essential elements of a 'pure' management contract can nevertheless be identified. In relation to these key features, other aspects may be viewed as merely minor variations on the central theme.

The CIRIA Report

The 1983 Construction Industry Research and Information Association (CIRIA) Report 100 on Management Contracting identified three areas in which management contracting (as it then stood) seemed more closely related to a professional service contract than to a normal construction contract. These were:

- the emphasis on management as a separate and contractually-defined discipline within the project;
- the payment mechanism (usually cost reimbursement plus fee); and
- the fact that the allocation of risk between client, management contractor and works contractors is significantly different from that in a conventional contract.

On the basis of its research in the industry, the CIRIA Report also identified a number of conditions which appeared to favour the use of a management contracting system. These indicate the concepts peculiar to management contracting and it is worth reciting them here:

'When there is a need for an early start to the construction phase. This may be required for political reasons, budgeting or procurement policy.

When there is a need for early completion of the project but the design is not sufficiently defined prior to construction. This circumstance requires good planning and control of the design/construction overlap and careful packaging of construction contracts.

When there is a need to consider particular construction methods during the design phase.

In complex projects and those involving high technology, management contracting can provide greater flexibility for design change than conventional contracts.

When the project is organisationally complex. Typically, this may arise from the need to manage and co-ordinate a considerable number of contractors and contractual interfaces and possibly several design organisations.

When the client and his advisers have insufficient management resources for the project.

When there are special features associated with the use of labour. For example, where there is a requirement to maximise the use of local firms and labour.'

The report continued by noting that the above circumstances do not of themselves provide a mandate for the adoption of management contracting. However, a combination of such circumstances may point to its selection as the most appropriate system for the project in question.

JCT Management Contract Practice Note MC/1

In the Practice Note MC/1 to the JCT Management Contract, management contracting is suggested as a suitable method of procurement where:

- the employer wants an independent design team;
- there is a need for early completion;
- the project is fairly large;
- the project requirements are complex;
- the project may entail changing the employer's requirements during the building period; and

- the employer while requiring early completion wants the maximum possible competition in respect of the price for the building works.

Essential features – cost, time and quality

It is perhaps possible to identify a number of essential features in a pure management contract by reference to the employer's three critical factors of cost, time and quality. ('Quality' is used in this context to mean the satisfactory performance of the project and, consequently, the availability of adequate remedies for defective performance.)

Cost

The contract will be priced on a cost reimbursement basis. The price will consist of reimbursement of prime cost plus a contractor's management fee, usually calculated on the basis of the prime cost. This calculation may be made at the outset by reference to estimated or budgeted prime cost and may or may not be recalculated later or adjusted according to the actual prime cost.

The estimated prices of the works contract packages to be let at a later stage make up the cost plan or estimate of the total contract price, rather than a fixed lump sum. The reimbursable prime cost mainly consists of the prices of the works contract packages sub-contracted by the management contractor. It also includes some preliminaries and other direct costs incurred by the management contractor. The management fee will normally allow for certain indirect costs as well as for the contractor's general overheads and profit.

The effects of management contracting on the cost of a project are various. It is outside the scope of a work of this nature to embark on an extended analysis of the balance of commercial advantage or disadvantage in such a system and most of the evidence is in any case anecdotal. However, some instances may be noted.

Fast track construction can lead to cost savings related to the contraction in the overall project period. The employer may be able to save interest on financing charges and, providing that the property market is buoyant, may be able to receive income from sale or letting of the property at an earlier time. There may be a reduction in site preliminaries and overheads.

The cost may also be reduced for some works contract packages by postponing tendering until nearer the time of execution of the work. This may be a difference of months or even years and should enable more precise estimating (even allowing for inflation). As each works package is let separately the employer should be able to obtain the best possible price for each element of the project. Tenders can be sought from specialist works contractors shortly before the works commence. Traditional main contractors have to estimate the cost of later works, perhaps many months before the works are actually required; this can sometimes lead to over-estimation of the cost of the works. In an inflationary economic climate, though, this may not necessarily benefit the employer.

The management fee should also be a smaller fraction of the prime cost than a traditional main contractor's profit/risk margin, given the intended low-risk nature of the system for the management contractor.

By contrast, the employer is sometimes thought to have less control over the build-up of prime cost, including the management contractor's preliminaries. Tighter time constraints may prejudice the employer's bargaining position when negotiating the costs of works contract packages, particularly if the sub-contracting of the packages has been left to a late stage in the project. There is inevitably less certainty at the outset of the overall cost to the employer.

Time

A considerable amount of time may be spent on carrying out a design in sufficient detail for tenders to be submitted for traditional main contracts. Management contracting should allow fast track construction, so that design and construction overlap. The detailed design of the project will not have been completed before construction begins. For example, tenders can be invited and works commenced in relation to ground works while the design of the plumbing system and other later works packages is continuing. This should reduce the overall period for the design and the construction of the project.

However, it should be noted that the professional team for the project does not necessarily have more time to carry out design; it is simply that construction of earlier elements of the work will have begun while the design of later elements continues. The effectiveness of attempts to save time and money by fast track construction depends very much on expert planning and programming of the project.

The construction period will be preceded by a pre-construction phase for planning, programming and commencement of design. Some works contract packages and orders may be placed during the pre-construction period but most will be let as the works proceed, relatively near the time the work for each has to be performed.

It is generally accepted that these time-related factors produce a shorter overall project period by telescoping the different phases of the programme, particularly by overlapping design and construction. The system is also said to lead to greater flexibility in accommodating variations to the works, because changes can be absorbed with minimal disruption to the programme. The exact nature of the employer's requirements will probably not be known when a management contractor is engaged. As each element of the project is treated as a separate works package and let at the latest stage possible, the knock-on effects of a change should be limited, particularly if it is made at an early stage of the project. However, it should be borne in mind that no procurement system can be totally flexible and that late changes in the project will affect schedules and costs.

An option to terminate the employment of the management contractor (a 'break clause') is frequently included and takes effect at the transition from pre-construction to construction period. However, operating this in practice may cause difficulties for the employer.

The management contractor will not bear full responsibility if the works contractors fail to finish in time. A mechanism will normally be introduced to make the management contractor's liability to pay liquidated damages for delay to the employer subject to his ability to recover liquidated damages from the works contractors.

Quality

The management contractor will have the opportunity, indeed the obligation, to be involved in the planning stages and (to a degree) the design of the project. He will at least have to advise on the 'buildability' of the design: that is, on the adaptability of the proposed design to operable methods and sequences of construction. The JCT package envisages the use of a separate design team. However, design and manage contracts are sometimes used, giving the management contractor responsibility for the design of the project as well as for managing the construction of it.

The management contractor will undertake little or no construction work himself but will sub-contract it to works contractors. The management contractor may himself be obliged to provide certain common facilities and attendances to works contractors or may sub-contract their provision as a separate works package.

Through some contractual mechanism, the management contractor will be relieved of liability to the employer for the performance (with regard to quality and defects) of the sub-contractors and for the risk of their being unable through insolvency to satisfy claims for defective performance.

Management contracts are usually intended to place a low degree of risk on the management contractor. The corollary, of course, is that they place on the employer a higher degree of risk than a traditional main contract. The mechanism which limits or excludes the management contractor's liability may affect the employer's overall remedies for defective performance or quality (see Chapter 11).

2 DISTINCTION FROM CONSTRUCTION MANAGEMENT

The essential features of a management contract described above are all subject to variation to a greater or lesser degree. Variants may be adopted for a number of reasons - to reflect alterations to the timing of a project; to modify the cost and fee structure or alter the relationship between fee and cost; or to change the distribution of risk between employer and management contractor (see Chapter 14).

However, the system has one structural feature whose variation turns the arrangement into something other than a management contract. In a management contract, the management contractor remains responsible for packaging the works to be performed by works contractors under works contracts. He also sub-contracts these works. The works contractors are all sub-contractors to the management contract. In other words, the principal contractual relationship for the works contractor is with the management contractor rather than the employer (though there will usually be separate collateral agreements between the employer and the works contractors).

If this structure is altered so that the employer rather than the management contractor directly contracts for the works contract packages, the entire tenor of the system is altered. It becomes a construction management system. (The expression 'construction management' is used in the USA to cover what in the UK are the two distinct concepts of management contracting and construction management.)

The essential feature of a construction management system is that, although the construction manager organises the splitting of the works into works contract packages, the employer engages with and employs the works contractors directly. Under this system the works contractors are usually known as trade contractors and works contracts are usually called trade contracts. The construction manager has a separate agreement with the employer, more akin to a professional consultancy than to a traditional main contract. This empowers him to act on behalf of the employer in dealing with the trade contractors. He may also be given responsibilities for procuring their performance. But under a construction management system, the construction manager (like the architect) does not intervene directly in the contractual chain between the employer and the trade contractors.

There is no published standard form in the UK for a construction management agreement or a related trade contract. However, construction management has become increasingly common in 'fast track' projects. It also received considerable impetus from its endorsement in the report of the 1991 University of Reading Forum for Construction Management (see Chapter 14). It is used particularly by large businesses that have a steady and consistent need for building procurement and so are able to accumulate a considerable degree of project management experience within their organisations. Businesses of this sort have developed their own forms of contract.

There are many sorts of construction management contract systems and this chapter is not intended to give a detailed account of them. However, it may be noted that even under a construction management agreement the construction manager may be required to assume some degree of responsibility for the trade contractors' workmanship and the quality of the materials they use, by acting as the supervisor of the trade contractors. The construction manager may also have to provide common facilities and attendances to trade contractors. However, some construction management systems may require the construction manager to take a measure of responsibility for the performance of trade contractors, either by being subject to liquidated damages for delayed completion or by being responsible for failing to procure construction which meets the specification. If this is the case, the construction manager will require his own direct agreements with trade contractors, giving him the right to procure from them work completed on time and of an acceptable standard. In these respects, the construction manager's position may be closer to a management contractor's than to that of a project manager, his counterpart in a purely professional consultancy relationship with the employer. The construction manager is in some respects a cross between a project manager and a management contractor.

It is noteworthy that there is a far wider choice of construction managers than management contractors. Management contracts contain obligations which could only realistically be accepted by main contractors. A prime example is the obligation to pay works contractors, which may not be dependent on the management contractor being paid by the employer. In contrast, professional firms are able to act as construction managers, if they have the necessary experience.

The employer will usually be able to change his construction manager (if necessary) without affecting the trade contracts and without any financial commitment beyond paying fees for work done up to the time of determination. A management contractor, by comparison, may be entitled to his entire projected profit if his employment is prematurely determined (as, for example, in Clauses 7.6 and 7.13 of JCT 87).

Finally, both management contracting and construction management systems are frequently adapted to give the management contractor or construction manager a partial or even total design responsibility. Variants abound, including design and management contracts; design, manage and construct contracts; and design and construction management contracts. These have the same relationship to a 'conventional' management contract or construction management agreement that a design and build agreement has to a traditional main contract. They are intended to maintain a single point of responsibility for the building procurement process (or at least its main aspects).

CHAPTER 5

FORMATION

1 INITIAL APPOINTMENT OF THE MANAGEMENT CONTRACTOR

To ensure that the maximum benefit of management contracting is achieved, the management contractor must be engaged at an early stage of the project, usually around the time that outline design proposals are finalised. However, it is not possible at such an early stage to agree conclusively all the matters which will have a bearing on the provision of the management contracting services. Consequently, the management contractor's initial appointment is often on a purely consultative basis and a formal management contract is not entered into until construction is due to commence. The initial appointment can take the form of a simple agreement to provide certain services in relation to overall planning of the project in return for an agreed fixed fee or on a time charge basis.

Pre-construction and construction periods

The Management Contract that is option F of the First Edition of the New Engineering Contract does not contemplate a formal pre-construction period as such, but it seems that some level of pre-construction services is required. For instance, certain information needs to be prepared and agreed by the parties before the Management Contract is executed. The guidance notes advise that if substantial pre-construction services are needed, a separate contract should be entered into between the parties in respect of these. The JCT Management Contract documentation proposes the use of a two-stage management contract which is divided into services before the commencement of construction (the pre-construction services) and services performed from the date on which the management contractor is given possession of the site (the construction services).

The essential items that need to be agreed when entering into an agreement for pre-construction consultative services with a management contractor are the scope of the consultative services and the fee that is to be paid for them. The JCT package assumes that the matters contained in the Appendix: Part 1 will be inserted (eg provisional dates for possession and completion, liquidated and ascertained damages and insurance policy details) and that a description of the project will be set out in the First Schedule. It is often not strictly necessary to agree all these details at such an early stage but it is best to agree on as many matters as possible to avoid future uncertainty and delays.

Although in theory it is necessary for there to be some division between the pre-construction and the construction periods, in practice the distinction is often blurred. Some elements of the work may be started before all the pre-construction services are performed and some pre-construction services may be carried out quite late into the construction stage.

In the JCT form, the pre-construction period ends on the proposed date of possession of the site stated in the Appendix: Part 1. However, the construction period does not begin until the management contractor takes possession of the site. There may therefore be an interval between the intended date of possession of the site and the actual date when the management contractor takes possession. This theoretically forms a lacuna during which the management contractor is not entitled to any fee.

Matters to be agreed before construction begins

Matters that need to be agreed before construction commences will be broadly similar in any form of management contract. Key elements of time, cost and how the project is to be carried out all need to be determined. The JCT Management Contract assumes that the matters set out in the Appendix: Part 2 will be agreed before construction commences. Additionally any amendments to the Third Schedule (services) and completion of the Fifth Schedule (facilities) should be agreed at the same stage with copies initialled as appropriate and with an appropriate entry made in the Appendix: Part 2.

Time

A date for possession, a date for completion, rates of liquidated and ascertained damages for delay, the defects liability period and a detailed programme for the project will all need to be agreed.

The programme is a particularly important document for a fast track project. It should show key periods for each work package (often more than just commencement and final completion dates), dates for release and return of information and the critical path of the project. In many non-standard forms of management contract, the programme is given the status of a contract document to ensure that failure to comply with it will be a breach of the management contract. The JCT Management

Contract does not do this, although it does contemplate that a detailed programme will be agreed between the parties.

Cost

A contract cost plan showing estimates of the prime cost of each works package needs to be prepared. This may also show the management contractor's estimate of the prime cost of any preliminaries that he is to provide on a reimbursable basis. The management contractor's fees need to be agreed as do the way in which they are to be paid and any formulae for adjusting them. If any of the management contractor's preliminary items are to be provided for a lump sum, this will also need to be agreed at this stage.

How the project is to be carried out

By the time the construction period begins, a description of the project in the form of drawings and specifications must have been prepared in enough detail for work to commence. The project will have been divided into elements which will provide the works packages for the works contracts; this needs to be done at an early stage of the pre-construction services to ensure effective cost planning and programming.

The exact scope of the management contractor's services also needs to be determined. The various insurance policies required for the project have to be taken out and details of such policies need to be incorporated in the management contract. The employer and management contractor must agree which site services and facilities are to be provided by the management contractor, and a prudent employer will agree with the management contractor which of the management contractor's personnel will be engaged on the project.

Refusal by the management contractor to agree

There is a risk to the employer in agreeing necessary details at a late stage. While the employer may be anxious to commence construction, the management contractor may be refusing to agree, for example, to an acceptable lump sum for site services. The employer is then in a position where he must either concede or anticipate a delay in commencement of construction while he negotiates with and appoints another management contractor and the new management contractor mobilises his resources. Even if the management contractor is being completely unreasonable in failing to agree the detail necessary for the completion of the management contract, it is unlikely that the employer will have redress against him, since English law will not generally enforce an agreement to agree. The House of Lords held in the case of *Walford v Miles* (1992) (which concerned the sale of a business) that the parties to a negotiation were not under a duty to continue negotiations in good faith. Such a duty would be inconsistent with the position of a negotiating party, since a party while negotiating should always be able to break off negotiations.

It has been suggested that, under the JCT Management Contract, the management contractor's failure to consent to details for the completion of the Appendix: Part 2 is a failure to proceed 'regularly and diligently with the carrying out of his obligations' under Clause 7.1.1 of the Management Contract. This could entitle the employer to issue a notice of default and termination allowing the employer a claim for direct loss or damage under Clause 7.4.4. But the fact remains that a management contractor cannot be compelled to proceed if he chooses not to and a court would not force him to do so.

2 PRE-CONSTRUCTION PERIOD – APPOINTMENT OF WORKS CONTRACTORS

To enable the employer's proposed date for completion to be achieved it may be necessary for a number of works contractors to be appointed during the pre-construction period. These may begin initial work such as demolition or ground works, or they may be specialist works contractors who are to assist the professional team with certain elements of the design.

Some forms of management contract, including the JCT package, contemplate that works contractors should be given final details of the management contract in their invitations to tender. Because these details will not all be available during the pre-construction period, there may be a conflict in the management contractor's obligations. For instance, the JCT system assumes that items from the Appendix: Part 2 of the Management Contract are set out in the invitation to tender. However, the management contractor is also under specific obligations to 'enter into works contracts in sufficient time to enable the Project to be duly carried out and completed on or before the Completion Date' (JCT Management Contract Clause 1.5.2). Under non-standard forms it may be possible to avoid these conflicts. Under the JCT Management Contract, the management contractor may be forced to ensure that the tendering requirements have been met by reissuing the invitation to tender to works contractors once the Appendix: Part 2 has been completed.

It should be noted that one of the advantages of construction management over management contracting is that, as the employer directly engages the trade contractors, the employer is able to engage specialists themselves at an early stage without engaging the construction manager. In such circumstances the employer does not need to consider arrangements for transferring contractual rights and obligations to the construction manager.

Supply of products and materials

Although it has been seen in the depressed building market of the late 1980s and early 1990s that the off-site production periods for certain products and materials can reduce as well as expand, it is still very important to ensure that such products with long lead-in times are ordered promptly. It may be necessary for orders to be placed for products and materials before a works contractor is engaged to fix them, so as to ensure that the overall programme for the project is not affected. In these circumstances it will be necessary for either the employer or the management contractor to enter into supply agreements with the supplier.

However, since the works contractor will eventually be responsible for handling and fixing the products, it may well be necessary to ensure that the supply agreements can be transferred to the works contractor. A tripartite novation agreement will be necessary to transfer both the right to receive the goods and the obligation to pay for the goods to the works contractor. Although it is in theory possible to require the supplier to confirm that he will agree to the future novation of the supply agreement to the works contractor, it is in practice necessary to ensure that the works contractor selected will accept novation of the supply agreement. He may be unwilling to do so if, for example, the supplier has already shown that he may not be able strictly to comply with the terms of the supply contract. In the JCT package the works contractor is likely to wish to ensure that such suppliers are treated as nominated suppliers for the purposes of Section 8 of Works Contract/2. In such circumstances it may be prudent when an advance order is being placed to agree that the supplier is willing to fulfil the conditions of Clause 8.3 of Works Contract/2.

An alternative is for the goods to be issued free to the works contractor for him to use in his works. In these circumstances the liability for the quality of the issued goods will remain with the person issuing them (the employer or management contractor) and a works contractor may seek express indemnities in relation to failure of the goods. If a defect becomes apparent in the works it is likely that a works contractor will try to show that it is due to a defect in the goods supplied and not a defect in workmanship in fixing the goods. The management contractor and the employer may then need to pursue remedies against both the works contractor and the supplier.

There are also practical difficulties in ordering goods before engaging works contractors. For instance, the correct amount of material must be ordered and the material ordered must be compatible with goods to be supplied by the works contractor.

3 BREAK CLAUSES

One of the features of the two-stage appointment procedure for a management contractor is that, if an employer is dissatisfied with the performance of a management contractor during the pre-construction period, he may choose not to proceed with that management contractor to the construction stage of the project.

Most first stage appointments for pre-construction services give the employer a right to terminate the management contractor's engagement on the project at the end of the pre-construction period without incurring further liability to the management contractor over and above the pre-construction fee. The employer usually has complete discretion as to whether to proceed or not, and the management contractor generally has no claim for breach of contract if the employer chooses not to proceed.

Under the JCT form, the management contractor has the right to payment of the balance of the pre-construction fee outstanding, but the employer is entitled to reduce this payment to take into account the extent to which the decision not to proceed is due to a fault of the management contractor (JCT Management Contract Clause 2.2). The provisions of Clause 2.2 as to how such deduction should be calculated are vague. The employer need not give reasons for any such decision not to proceed. However, if an employer wishes to make a deduction from the pre-construction fee payable to the management contractor it would be prudent for him to keep records as to why he believed a deduction was justified and how he calculated the amount of the deduction.

In practice it is likely that during the pre-construction stage the management contractor will have entered into some works contracts and possibly some supply agreements. It is therefore in the employer's interest to ensure that any such contracts and agreements contain provisions allowing them to be transferred to the employer or another management contractor if the contract is terminated.

A clause requiring the management contractor to transfer his interest will also be required. Such a clause is included as Clause 7.11.2 of the JCT Management Contract. However, it should be noted that the clause used there provides for transfer of the agreements by assignment; that is, transfer of the benefit of the agreement but not the burden. If the employer later defaults in payment to the works contractor or supplier, the management contractor may have a residual liability to pay the works contractor or supplier.

Clause 7.11.2 of the JCT Management Contract also allows the works contractor or supplier to object to a further assignment. The employer, therefore, may engage a new management contractor but the works contractor or supplier may refuse to transfer his obligations. Clause 2.2 of the JCT Management Contract provides that there is a 'deemed determination' of the management contractor's employment where the employer issues a notice not to proceed or fails to issue a notice to proceed within the prescribed periods. It is questionable whether the structure of the JCT Management Contract allows the provisions of Clause 7.11 to be applied to such determination. It may however be that the provisions should be applied as the deemed determination is a determination under Clauses 7.10 and 7.12 – a determination at will by the employer before the construction period.

A prudent management contractor will require the employer to indemnify him against claims made by works contractors for amounts that have not been paid to the management contractor by the employer and which are due to the works contractors if a break clause is operated. An example of wording dealing with such an eventuality can be found in Clause 7.11.1 of the JCT Management Contract.

In view of these problems and the likely time and cost consequences, an employer will only wish to operate such a break clause if he has very strong reservations about proceeding with a particular management contractor.

4 EUROPEAN COMMUNITY LEGISLATION

As is the case for any construction contract, before the management contract and related contracts are entered into, the parties should consider the requirements of European Community law. Here we mention briefly some points to bear in mind; a more detailed consideration is beyond the scope of this book.

If the works in question are of a public sector nature, the public procurement directives and the regulations implementing those directives in this country must be followed. These attempt to ensure effective competition and transparency during the letting of public contracts. So, for example, discrimination on non–objective grounds, particularly because of nationality, is prohibited. Another factor is that contracts are to be awarded on the basis of lowest price and most economically advantageous tender.

The European Community requirements for health and safety at temporary or mobile construction sites should also be considered. At present, draft regulations (which are expected to come into force in 1994) set out the duties that arise. For example, a health and safety plan is to be drawn up for each project, indicating the approach towards managing health and safety in connection with that project, and identifying hazards and precautionary measures. The employer is required to appoint a planning supervisor, who has initial responsibility for the health and safety plan, and a 'principal contractor', who later takes responsibility for the plan. The draft regulations impose duties on all concerned - employer, planning supervisor, principal contractor, designers and all other contractors - to see that statutory health and safety requirements are complied with and that sufficient resources are devoted to that task.

CHAPTER 6

OPERATION

1 NATURE OF THE MANAGEMENT OBLIGATION

An important feature that distinguishes management contracting from traditional forms of building contract is the series of obligations placed on the management contractor to manage the works rather than carrying them out himself.

In traditional main building contracts the architect or engineer takes the lead in managing the contract and the works. In management contracting some of the burden for management is placed on the management contractor. Managing a project involves planning, control and co-ordination of the project from inception to completion. This is necessary to meet the employer's requirements and ensure completion on time, within cost and to required quality standards.

The management contractor, however, is not in charge of the overall project. He still takes instructions from the architect or contract administrator. An employer who uses a management contract form should recognise that although management contracting may give him more flexibility and a less costly and more quickly-completed project, it also means that he has to provide a larger amount of management control himself. An employer using a pure form of management contracting carries a far greater proportion of the risk than he would do in traditional main contracting and it is in his interest to ensure that the risks are controlled.

The management contractor's obligations

The primary obligation on a management contractor in most forms of management contract is to manage the carrying out and completion of the project. This is often accompanied by references to concepts of organisation, supervision and procurement which are intended to elaborate on the management function. The procedures contained in the management contract and the services which it requires the management contractor to perform also indicate the scope of the management contractor's obligation. It is impossible to draw up a definitive list of every management function in every management contract. There must be some element of choice in the drafting of the contract to facilitate the selection of an appropriate course of action in any given situation. (It should be noted in this context that the JCT Management Contract provides for the list of services in the Third Schedule to be amended by agreement during the pre-construction period.)

Pre-construction period

During the pre-construction phase, the management undertaken by the management contractor will include a contribution to the planning of the project. He must then ensure that procedures planned in the pre-construction stage are used (with any variations that are necessary) to achieve the time, cost and quality targets.

Planning a project will typically involve the management contractor carrying out or collaborating in the following activities:

- programming;
- cost planning;
- division of works into works packages; and
- selection and procurement of works contractors.

The management contractor will be expected to prepare proposals for working methods and procedures and to draw up procedures for site control and safety. He will probably also be required to assist in making insurance arrangements. The provision of such services will involve close co-operation with the professional team, to establish fully the criteria of time, cost and quality in accordance with the employer's needs for the project and then to propose ways of achieving these criteria, making the best use of available resources.

Construction period

The construction services should always overlap with the pre-construction services. Particularly in a fast track project, not all matters will be fully planned before construction starts and construction services such as monitoring the works contractors' off-site preparation will begin in the pre-construction period.

A typical example of the principal construction obligation placed on a management contractor is found in Article 1.2 of the JCT Management Contract, which says that the management contractor must

'... set out, manage, organise, supervise and secure the carrying out and completion of the Project on or before the Date of Completion or such other date as may be fixed under the Conditions inclusive of all such works or items of work as are to be carried out under and in accordance with the Works Contracts which the Management Contractor is required to enter into hereunder.'

This obligation is elaborated upon in Clause 1.5 of the conditions of the JCT Management Contract and is supplemented by a requirement to carry out the services listed in the Third Schedule (Clause 1.6).

The general range of construction services which a management contractor would be required to perform includes the following elements:

- planning, control, co-ordination and administration of the works and the works contracts;
- monitoring the work carried out as regards standards and progress;
- monitoring expenditure against cost plans, making cash flow projections and keeping full accounts;
- collecting and distributing project information;
- site control – including such matters as health and safety, industrial relations, control of noise and waste emissions, access, security and relations with any third parties likely to be affected by the project;
- attending meetings and making reports;
- managing disputes between and with works contractors; and
- collating information on completion of the project.

Allocation of risk

It is important to emphasise that in pure management contract forms the employer undertakes much of the risk which under traditional main contracts falls on the main contractor. This is often said to place the management contractor in the role of a consultant – a professional manager – who, without the burden of risk, is in a position to manage the project in the employer's best interests. However, some commentators have suggested that the opposite is true: that while the management contractor is relieved of risk he is also relieved from the commercial incentive to manage since he is not the person ultimately responsible if the management technique fails. While this may be true to an extent, a management contractor is still open to liability for negligence if he fails in or is careless in fulfilling his management role (subject to the provisions in the form of management contract relieving him of liability, discussed in Chapter 11).

Co-operation

Co-operation and co-ordination between the consultants for a project has long been recognised as a responsibility of the professional team. If the management contractor is to be seen as at least a quasi-consultant, some form of obligation will be placed upon him to co-operate with the professional team.

Different management contracts place varying emphasis on co-operation. Most forms at least require that certain duties are carried out in collaboration with the professional team or that assistance is given to the team in carrying out certain aspects of its duties. The JCT gives prominence to the management contractor's duty to co-operate; the third recital of the JCT Management Contract states that the employer and the management contractor have agreed that the management contractor will 'co-operate with the professional team'. Similar wording appears in Article 1.1 and Clause 1.4 of the JCT Management Contract.

The emphasis in the JCT form contrasts with that in traditional forms of main contract. It has been established in case law that traditional forms of contract impose an obligation on each party to the contract not to hinder or prevent the other from performing its obligations. However, they have not been held to imply any positive duties on the contractor.

In *Holland Hannen & Cubitts (Northern) Ltd v Welsh HTFO* (1981) the judge discussed the scope of co-operation between an architect and a traditional main building contractor. The main discussion was focused on the architect's duties and not those of the contractor who - once he had made known his requirements for detailed drawings - was viewed as a passive recipient of information.

The nature of the project

When defining the duties which the management contractor is to perform, it is necessary to consider the nature of the project to be carried out. For instance, the duties necessary for the construction of an industrial unit on a green field site will not be entirely the same as those required for fitting out a city-centre office building. The JCT recognised this in drawing up its Management Contract and specifically anticipated that the parties would amend the list of services contained in the Third Schedule. In using any form of management contract the exact scope of the services required for the particular project needs to be considered carefully and will need to be dovetailed with the services performed by the professional team.

Personnel

The quality and quantity of management given to a project is important. The personalities of those carrying out the management function are crucial and most forms of management contract recognise this by requiring that key personnel who will be involved in the project are named. It is in an employer's interest when selecting a management contractor to interview the employees who will be responsible for the project to ensure that he has confidence in their individual ability to manage.

2 DESIGN OBLIGATIONS

The management contractor's design obligations

Under many forms of management contract, the management contractor has only limited design responsibility. His duties will often be chiefly supervisory - as under the JCT Management Contract. The professional team will have prime responsibility for the design with the works contractors perhaps having responsibility for particular aspects.

Under a standard management contract, such as the JCT form, the management contractor co-operates with the professional team as to design, but is not responsible for it. Article 1.1 of the JCT Management Contract provides for his co-operation during the design stage. The management contractor also receives copies of all drawings from the architect but has no responsibility for their content (JCT Management Contract Clause 1.10).

Buildability and value engineering

The management contractor's construction expertise should allow him to advise to some degree on design. He may comment on the availability and selection of goods and materials, advise on construction methods, and give advice about the buildability of proposed designs and (possibly) about value engineering.

The management contractor advises on buildability after evaluating the designs of the professional team. He uses his expertise as a contractor to assess whether the designs can be achieved given the available construction techniques, the budget and cost plan, and the proposed timetable for the works. He may recommend ways in which the architect's design can be realised more easily; he does not change the design.

Value engineering is a creative technique designed to increase the value of the project by identifying the needs or function of a particular item and then offering alternatives to meet the same requirements at a lower cost. It requires a higher level of expertise and input from the relevant designers and specialist sub-contractors than advice on buildability.

The JCT Management Contract Third Schedule provides that the management contractor will advise on buildability (paragraph 4) and 'on the practical implications of proposed drawings and specifications' (paragraph 3). It therefore appears that buildability advice is required but that a value engineering exercise is not envisaged.

Responsibility for works contractor's designs

The Third Schedule of the JCT Management Contract does not include in its list of services to be provided by the management contractor a specific reference to the management contractor's responsibility for the works contractor's designs. The JCT Management Contract merely requires the management contractor to monitor the progress of all works contractors and suppliers in producing design work and working drawings and to report on them to the professional team (paragraph 20). The management contractor also secures the provision of record drawings from works contractors (paragraph 53).

Non-standard management contracts place varying degrees of responsibility on the management contractor for the procurement and co-ordination of the designs of works contractors. Normally, however, a management contractor will have little responsibility. In most contractor-generated forms of management contract, the management contractor's express duties in respect of a works contractor's design are limited to acting as a clearing-house, receiving drawings and specifications from the professional team and works contractors and passing them on to the appropriate party. Indeed, it is not uncommon for there to be an express disclaimer for any responsibility for design.

Some employers believe that, as the management contractor has the primary contractual link with the works contractors, he should have a more active role in the management of the design. The JCT form gives the management contractor insufficient control in this regard. It seems sensible for the management contractor to have at least some role in co-ordinating the timely supply of design information by the works contractors and in programming the exchange of information between the professional team and the works contractors so that the project is not delayed. If the management contractor's role is to be extended in this way, any list of the management services he provides will need amending (for example in the Third Schedule to the JCT Management Contract).

The employer may also wish the management contractor to have some influence on the content of the design. Some forms of management contract go so far as to require from the management contractor a degree of review of the works contractor's design information and the cross-checking of drawings to ensure that, for example, there are no conflicts between the designs of the various elements of the works.

Overview of management contractor's obligations

The management contractor in many forms of management contract takes no real responsibility for design. His role is peripheral to that of the professional team and works contractors. If the employer wants to impose added responsibilities on the management contractor, he will have to amend a typical contract such as the JCT Management Contract. An extreme version would be a design and management contract, with the management contractor doing the detailed design as well as managing construction.

Even in a standard management contract, the combination of the management contractor's duties in respect of works contractors and his preliminary advice on buildability and value engineering mean that he sometimes crosses the nebulous divide between design and construction services and is likely to be seen as having some responsibility for the design of the project. In addition, although the management contractor does not prepare final plans and specifications and lacks control over the design process, the architect and employer are in part relying on his expertise. Negligence may therefore lead to tortious liability.

Design obligations of the architect and design team

In theory, the design for each works contract package need not be completed until just before tenders are issued for that specific package. The design can be produced while the contract is underway. However, the fast track nature of management contracting means that the design team may have only a short time in which to produce the design.

Design under a management contract requires good administration by the architect, because of the added complexity created by overlapping activities. For example, buildability studies will start before design is settled in principle. Actual work on site may begin before detailed planning approvals have been obtained. The design team in the early days will be large, as people work in parallel, some producing information for different works packages while others oversee the employer's interests and document production. It is up to the architect to run the design programme and his team.

The design team's duties include providing enough design information at the right time to enable the works contractor to start his detailed design in good time. The team should also comment on the works contractor's design drawings within a reasonable period. Another point for the architect and design team to bear in mind is that the management contractor has the opportunity to give his opinion on the design, and comment on it in relation to buildability.

The employer's contractual remedies for design defects depend on the conditions of engagement between the employer and the professional team responsible for the design. If a third party designed or contributed to the design, the specific contractual arrangements between the employer and that third party will have to be considered.

3 ADMINISTRATION OF THE MANAGEMENT CONTRACT

Although the management contractor may have a consultative and professional role within a project, he is still under the administrative control of the contract administrator (usually the architect) and, to a lesser extent, the other members of the professional team and the employer. It should be noted that the standard forms of professional appointment as published by the various professional bodies do not specifically contemplate the use of management contracting as a method of procurement. When agreeing the engagement of the members of the professional team for any given project, it may well be necessary to consider their terms of appointment with regard to their roles in administering a management contract.

The architect or contract administrator

In any form of management contract, many powers and duties will be assigned to the architect, enabling him to administer the contract. These will affect almost all aspects of the management contractor's services. In this respect, the management contractor will not be on an equal footing with the professional team.

The architect often has the role of a supervising officer, as he does in traditional building contracts. Under the JCT Management Contract, and with many non-standard forms of management contract, the architect has a wider discretion in issuing instructions than he has under traditional building contract forms, where he is often restricted to giving instructions in relation to certain specified matters. Under the JCT Management Contract he has a duty to issue 'such instructions as are reasonably necessary to enable the management contractor properly to discharge his obligations' (Clause 3.3.1). This duty has been phrased in an objective manner: the architect must issue whatever instructions are reasonably necessary. The management contractor's duty to co-operate with the professional team seems to imply that he may request from the architect instructions which it is 'reasonably necessary' for him to receive before he can properly discharge his obligations. It also suggests that he may discuss with the architect the scope of the instructions to be given.

Other forms of management contract may place greater reliance on the architect's choice of whether an instruction is necessary. They may even give him total discretion as to the instructions to be issued (for example, 'the architect may issue such instructions as he thinks fit in connection with the project') although restrictions on the architect's authority may be imposed through the terms of his appointment.

As well as having a general power and obligation to issue necessary instructions, the architect will have discretion to issue instructions for the control of the project in specific circumstances (opening up work for inspection, for instance, or testing goods and materials). Such specific powers assume more importance in the JCT Management Contract, where the works contractors are able to call upon the architect to specify the provision of the Management Contract which empowers the issue of any given instruction. The management contractor under the JCT form (and many non-standard forms of management contract) is not given an express right to challenge instructions. It seems that, insofar as work contractors are able to challenge instructions, the management contractor in the JCT form acts as a channel of communications between the architect and the works contractors.

The architect finally decides what instructions are issued, but there should be co-operation between the management contractor and the professional team so that problems can be solved in the employer's best interests and full use can be made of the management contractor's construction expertise.

The architect's supervisory role is perhaps more complex in a management contracting system than in other systems. He needs not only to be aware of the operation of one main contract but also to be able to make decisions in the light of conditions affecting each of the works contracts. If extensions of time are considered, he must assess whether a particular works contractor has been delayed by a cause which would entitle him to an extension of time or by his own default. Only in the first instance should the management contractor be granted an extension under the management contract. Where there are a number of reasons for a delay and more than one works contractor is affected this can be a time-consuming and difficult exercise.

The employer

Although the employer cannot usually issue instructions directly to the management contractor, he still has powers and duties under the management contract (relating, for instance, to provision of the site, payment, insurance and determination of the management contract). Additionally, of course, he will make decisions affecting the instructions which the architect issues under the management contract.

The quantity surveyor

The quantity surveyor assumes a role that is similar to his role under traditional building contracts. Generally he sets the cost parameters for the project in the cost plan (with assistance from the professional team and the management contractor). The architect calls upon the quantity surveyor to prepare valuations to form the basis of interim certificates. However, his role is a more complex one as he is involved in ascertaining loss or expense under works contracts (see, for example, Clause 8.5 of the JCT Management Contract). He must have a good knowledge of possible contra-charges between each of the works contractors to enable him to exclude from certificates costs arising from the management contractor's negligence or from defaults by works contractors.

Under traditional forms of building contract, the quantity surveyor will often leave the administration of contra-charges between sub-contractors to the main contractor. In the final analysis, the quantity surveyor's decision on amounts payable to works contractors prevails over that of the management contractor. In this sense, they cannot truly be said to be equal members of the project team.

Certificates

Certificates under management contracts are generally issued by the architect to the employer and copied to the management contractor. When dealing with the payment certificates, as noted above, the architect will rely on information prepared by the quantity surveyor. Certificates relating to completion are also usually issued by the architect and (as in most forms of traditional building contract) it is within his discretion to issue or withhold certificates, subject to his duty to act fairly.

4 STANDARD OF CARE

In management contracting, the management contractor, the works contractors, the architect and other designers all supply services of various sorts. These services may include, for example, management, supervision, design, building or programming. In addition, goods and materials are supplied, often by the works contractor. What level of skill and care must be devoted to the supply of these services? What standards must the goods and materials meet?

Implied terms

Implied terms as to the supply of goods and services are laid down in Section 4 (goods) and Section 13 (services) of the Supply of Goods and Services Act 1982. These implied terms apply if they are not displaced by different express contractual terms. In addition, case law suggests that in some circumstances, and on certain facts, more onerous terms may be implied.

As to goods, the Section 4 warranty is that they will be of merchantable quality - that is, reasonably fit for the purpose for which goods of that kind are commonly supplied. In addition, provided the particular purpose for which the goods are being acquired is made known to the supplier and provided it is not shown that the client did not rely on the skill or judgment of the supplier, the goods are to be reasonably fit for that particular purpose. The case of *University of Warwick v Sir Robert McAlpine* (1988) makes clear that fitness for particular purpose applies only if there is actual reliance. 'Fitness for purpose' imposes a strict liability. There will be no need to prove that the builder failed to exercise reasonable skill and care if it is clear that the materials were simply not fit for their purpose.

As to services, the implied warranty, contained in s 13, is that reasonable care and skill will be exercised. This means no more than the ordinary skill of the ordinary competent and relevantly-qualified man performing those obligations and services.

Exceptionally, the courts are prepared to imply a higher standard for the provision of services. For example, where there is a design and build or 'package deal' contract, there may be an implied warranty that the finished product will be fit for the purpose for which it was required or that the design itself must be fit for the purpose (*Greaves & Co (Contractors) Ltd v Baynham, Meikle & Partners* (1975)). The courts may find, by analogy with the sale of goods, that a completed structure is to be fit for the purpose (*Independent Broadcasting Authority v EMI Electronics Ltd and BICC Construction Ltd* (1978)).

The courts are generally reluctant to accept the argument that, because the supplier possessed exceptional expertise and experience, he should have exercised a higher degree of competence and care. This argument is relevant for the management contractor, who should have higher programming and management skills than the average contractor. It is a matter of looking at the facts of the case. Did the client reasonably expect superior service? Was the client contracting for a particular result or level of achievement, and not just for the supply of competent professional services?

If the management contract documents contain no express terms covering the standard of care to be expected, the duties of the parties are therefore as follows. Where any services are supplied, whether by the management contractor, the works contractor or the architect, reasonable care and skill must be exercised. This would apply, for example, to the management contractor's duties of supervision, programming or selection of materials; to the works contractor's design and building work; and to the architect's design and inspection. On occasion, it may be possible to argue, on the facts, that a higher standard should apply. Any goods supplied are to be fit for the purpose for which such goods are commonly supplied and also fit for a particular purpose where that purpose was made known. The works contractor is the party most likely to supply goods.

Where the contract is silent on standard of care, the inexperienced employer may not realise that the management contractor's duty of care is only to use reasonable skill and care rather than his best endeavours – at least until problems arise for which the employer believes the management contractor is to blame. It is difficult for the employer to measure the quality of the management contractor's work. The result of a contractual claim against the management contractor for breach of obligations to exercise care and skill in performance of services must be uncertain, because there is no established standard in English law against which the level of care and skill required of a management contractor can be judged.

Express terms

The contract documents may impose higher or lower standards, depending on which party had the upper hand in negotiating. Clearly, the employer will try to impose the highest possible standard, while the management or works contractor will try to reduce his potential liability by arguing for nothing more than a standard of reasonable skill and care. A non-standard form prepared for the employer might require the management contractor to exercise all the skill, care and diligence of a properly-qualified competent manager, acting in the best interests of the employer and experienced in managing and carrying out work of a similar size, scope, nature, value and complexity to the work now in question.

Under the JCT 87 contracts, there is no specific provision dealing with how the management contractor or the architect is to carry out the supply of services. The various contract documents do, however, contain provisions which set out the standards that goods, workmanship and design must attain. The JCT Management Contract stipulates compliance with certain standards, making the management contractor technically liable to the employer if at the end of the day the construction does not meet these standards. In reality, however, these are obligations to be met by the works contractor. The provisions are considered in Chapter 8, Section 2.

As is explained in detail in Chapter 11 below, there are potential problems with claims by the employer against works contractors, where these must be made via the management contractor. It may therefore be advisable to impose obligations on the works contractor, by a direct employer/works contractor agreement. The agreement might provide an absolute performance obligation, rather than a duty to exercise reasonable skill and care.

'State of the art' defence

Where a design is defective, but was generally in accordance with accepted practice when designed and the particular weakness was not known at the time, the designer, whether he is the architect, the works contractor or a third party, may be able to plead a 'state of the art' defence. The argument will be that no one in the industry would have foreseen the problem. However, if the designer uses untried materials, he must warn the employer and let him approve their use, otherwise he may be guilty of negligence. In addition, a state of the art defence cannot assist a designer who has warranted that the design will be fit for its purpose.

5 INSURANCE

As with any form of building contract, the apportionment of risk by means of insurance and indemnification is an important matter in management contracting. The risks that each party – the management contractor, the works contractor and the employer – may be open to and how these will be borne or insured need to be addressed at a very early stage of a project. It is important that the employer seeks advice from his insurance brokers to assist in identifying risks and determining how they are to be covered.

JCT Practice Notes MC/1 and MC/2 describe the insurance regime under the JCT 87 system. This represents one method of apportioning risk by insurance. Non-standard forms apportion liability for and obligations to insure risks in a different manner. The risks that typically need to be considered are listed below. (This is not an exhaustive list, and for any given project there may be other risks that need to be addressed.) Risks include:

- loss or damage to the works;
- loss or damage to any existing structures on the site;
- liability to third parties
  - arising from death or personal injury, and
  - arising from damage to property;
- liability to employees of the management contractor or works contractors for death or personal injury;
- loss or damage to plant or equipment used in carrying out the works; and
- losses arising from negligent performance of professional or design obligations.

Loss or damage to the works

The JCT Management Contract assumes that the management contractor will insure the works and materials which are on the site for incorporation into the works in the joint names of the management contractor and the employer. The policy either recognises each works contractor as a joint insured or contains a waiver of subrogation rights against him. The employer bears the cost of the insurance, which is reimbursable as an item of prime cost. He also covers the excess on any claim, as any reinstatement work carried out by works contractors is treated as a variation and is therefore paid by the employer as part of the prime cost.

Non-standard forms of management contracts commonly require the employer to take out and maintain insurance against loss or damage to the works in the joint names of himself, the management contractor and the works contractors. This has the following advantages for the employer:

- he can start detailing insurance arrangements at an early stage, even before he has finally decided which management contractor to engage;

- he can be sure that premiums have been paid;
- if the management contract is determined the employer will not need to consider new insurance arrangements but may simply alter the existing policy;
- the early construction packages will not be delayed while insurance arrangements are made by the management contractor; and
- claims will not fall between different works contractors' insurers.

In some non-standard forms the employer continues to bear the excess. In others, he may choose to place the burden of the excess on the management contractor (although this may be seen as contrary to the low-risk philosophy of pure management contracting) or to place it on the management contractor insofar as the loss or damage is caused by the default of the management contractor or his works contractors. While this seems a more equitable solution, time and cost would have to be spent on establishing liability for any given damage.

Loss or damage to existing structures

Under a management contract, as under most other forms of contract, existing structures on the site are usually insured by the employer.

Where the employer is insuring the works, his insurance of existing structures will often be under the same policy and subject to similar conditions. If the management contractor is insuring the works and works are not being carried out to the existing structures themselves, or there are structures adjoining or close to the site which may be affected by the works, the employer may wish the management contractor to insure against some of the risks arising out of the works (such as collapse or subsidence) in respect of the existing structures and adjoining property (so-called 'non-negligence' insurance). Clause 6.11 of the JCT Management Contract provides an example of such an insurance clause. The insurance is of a similar kind to that which the employer can require the contractor to maintain under Clause 21.2.1 of JCT 80.

Liability to third parties

Management contractors generally take responsibility for public liability risks. They usually indemnify the employer against risks of death or personal injury, to the extent that these do not arise from the actions or neglect of the employer. The indemnity usually covers damage to property to the extent that it arises through the management contractor's fault (which includes the works contractors' fault).

The indemnities given are usually counterbalanced by indemnities from the works contractors and coupled with insurance obligations. In many cases the management contractor insures and is also obliged to see that his works contractors take out insurance in respect of liability to third parties. Where the employer has opted to take out a single project policy or a project insurance programme he is likely to provide the insurance coverage for these risks on a joint names policy basis but may still require indemnification from the management contractor. An alternative is that the employer may require the management contractor to take out a joint names policy for the management contractor and the employer, and indemnify the employer to the extent that the damage has not arisen by reason of the employer's default.

Liability to employees

In common with most other forms of management contract, the JCT Management Contract (Clause 6.10.1) requires the management contractor to maintain insurances which comply with the Employer's Liability (Compulsory Insurance) Act 1969 and any supplementary legislation to the Act in respect of personal injury to, or the death of, any person employed by him or under apprenticeship with him, and to ensure that his works contractors similarly maintain such insurance.

Loss or damage to plant or equipment

A number of different arrangements can exist between the management contractor and the employer for the insurance of plant and equipment. Any plant or equipment that belongs to a works contractor or of which he has possession or control is usually at the works contractor's risk, except to the extent that the loss or damage is caused by the management contractor or someone else for whom – as between himself and the works contractor – the management contractor is responsible (for example, the employer or other works contractors). Some forms of works contract require the works contractor to ensure that such plant and equipment is insured but others leave this to the individual works contractor's discretion. The philosophy behind this is that, if the employer or management contractor insures the risk of loss or damage to the works contractor's plant, there is less incentive for the works contractor to take care of or protect his own plant. In any event, the works contractor is likely to maintain insurance for his own equipment.

If the management contractor is either supplying plant for the works or carrying out part of the works, the obligation to insure is sometimes assumed by the employer, particularly if he has taken out a single project policy. In such circumstances it is likely that certain equipment will be excluded (eg motor vehicles) and that the coverage will not extend to breakdown or failure of equipment. Other forms are silent on the subject, except in that they exclude plant and equipment from any definition of items covered by the works insurance and public liability insurance, so that any loss lies where it falls (that is, with the management contractor).

Losses arising from negligent performance of professional or design obligations

A prudent employer will ensure that his management contractor has and agrees to maintain professional indemnity insurance like every other member of the professional team. It is becoming increasingly common for specialist design works contractors also to be required to obtain and maintain this insurance in respect of their design obligations.

Professional indemnity insurance is generally taken out on an annual basis and on a claims-made basis. In other words, it responds to claims made during the year that it is in force, not to future claims made in respect of duties carried out negligently during that year. It is therefore important that the obligation to maintain insurance is a continuing one. The insurance is for the benefit of the insured – the management contractor or works contractor – to protect them against proven claims of negligence. The comfort that an employer receives from knowing that the insurance is in place is that (subject to the terms and limitations of the insurance) there is sure to be money available to meet a claim if he can prove negligence.

It is unlikely that an employer would be able effectively to enforce an obligation to maintain professional indemnity insurance without some other claim being available to him for negligence on the part of the management contractor. If the employer has no claim in negligence for a breach of duty which would be insured under the policy, he will probably have no substantial loss arising from the failure to insure. If there is a proven claim for negligence and no insurance is in place, it may be that there are insufficient assets to meet the claim for negligence and that an action for breach of the obligation to insure will thus not aid the employer. Because of this, under some forms of management contract, if the management contractor fails to provide evidence that insurance is being maintained, the employer has the right to take out insurance on behalf of the management contractor and either to deduct the cost of the premiums from monies due to the management contractor or recover these as debt from him. (Similar rights are also found in relation to other kinds of insurance required to be maintained under management contracts.)

6 VARIATIONS

The management contractor is not in charge of the overall project; the architect or contract administrator retains the power to issue instructions to the management contractor. These may alter or modify the scope of the project, affecting a number of works contract packages, or they may affect only one works package.

The JCT form distinguishes between project changes – which alter or modify the scope of the project as shown and described generally in the project drawings and specification – and works contract variations. However, no special provisions apply to project changes. It seems likely that the definition of the term is included merely to establish beyond doubt that the architect may issue instructions which alter or modify the scope of the entire project.

The management contractor will usually be under an obligation to comply with (or secure compliance with) instructions issued by the architect. But under the JCT form, a works contractor is not required to comply with an instruction to vary the works to the extent that he makes a reasonable written objection to compliance. Where the instruction would affect the works contractor's obligations in relation to design, selection of goods and materials or satisfaction of any performance specification, his written consent (which he cannot unreasonably delay or withhold) is necessary before he is obliged to comply with the instruction (Clause 3.4.1 of JCT Works Contract/2, the works contract conditions).

Clause 1.8 of the JCT Management Contract releases the management contractor from the obligation to secure compliance if the works contractor reasonably objects or (where relevant) withholds consent. In addition, either the management contractor or a works contractor may object to instructions to accelerate or to work out of sequence (see below).

Management contractor's directions

Some works contracts (including the JCT form) allow the management contractor to issue 'directions' to works contractors without any instruction from the architect. This is in addition to and separate from the architect's right to issue an instruction to vary the works of a single works contractor. A direction may arise from matters for which the employer is responsible but will frequently reflect the need to modify the works as a result of the delay or default of the management contractor himself or of another works contractor.

Valuation of variations

Management contracts do not generally depart from the traditional method by which the quantity surveyor values variations instructed by the architect. In common with most non-standard forms, the Third Schedule to the JCT Management Contract makes the management contractor responsible for providing a cost estimate if a variation instructed by the architect will result in an adjustment to any lump sum payable to the management contractor himself. Non-standard forms sometimes require the management contractor to agree the cost of variations instructed by the architect with works contractors before implementation.

Where the management contractor has issued a direction to a works contractor, valuation is generally the responsibility of the quantity surveyor to the extent that payment is the responsibility of the employer. In general, the value of variations affecting the works contract packages will form part of the reimbursable prime cost of the project. Where the variation affects the services provided by the management contractor himself, he will usually be entitled either to recover the value of the variation as prime cost or to seek an adjustment of any lump sum payable in respect of his services. However, there may be circumstances in which the management contractor has agreed to bear certain risks himself or where a cap (which may or may not be capable of adjustment to reflect the particular variation) applies. Responsibility both for valuation and for payment in respect of directions arising out of the delay or default of the management contractor or of another works contractor rests with the management contractor, as does the application of any set-off which may be appropriate (see Section 8).

Non-standard forms of contract may incorporate an overall cost ceiling or cap, based on the target cost plan but adjustable in certain circumstances. Where costs are capped in this way, it is normally the responsibility of the management contractor to make any necessary application and provide the information or cost estimates required to secure an adjustment of the cap figure so as to allow for the financial effect of the variation.

Acceleration and altering sequence or timing of works

Variation provisions in management contracts broadly reflect those of the traditional contract, by which the employer has the right to instruct a variation and the management contractor is required to comply or (subject to the benefit of any relieving provisions) to secure compliance. The management contractor is entitled to reimbursement and (where appropriate) to an extension of time in accordance with the terms of the contract.

An exception to this general rule is the optional provision of the JCT Management Contract (Clause 3.6) which entitles the architect to issue an instruction to accelerate or to alter the sequence or timing of the works. This clause provides a framework within which the employer (through the architect or contract administrator), the management contractor and works contractors can agree to acceleration or resequencing and to the financial and other adjustments to the contract which result. In some ways this is little more than a formalisation of the type of acceleration agreement which is in practice often made where works are carried out under forms of contract with no provisions for acceleration. Clause 3.6 and Clauses 3.4.2 to 3.4.7 of JCT Works Contract/2 require that the objections (if any) and proposals of the management contractor and works contractors with regard to acceleration or resequencing should be reasonable (an arbitration can be opened on this point before practical completion). In practice, however, it is unlikely that this provision would operate so as actually to secure an acceleration in the face of objections from the management contractor or works contractors. The acceleration provisions in the JCT 87 package are discussed further in Chapter 7, Section 8.

7 LOSS AND EXPENSE CLAIMS

Under a cost reimbursement form of contract, there is no obvious reason to provide for payment of loss and expense. The question of loss and expense will however arise in relation to the works contract packages, which are tendered on a lump sum basis. Where the management contractor's own services are provided on a lump sum rather than a pure cost reimbursable basis, it is also likely that the formula for adjustment of the lump sum will in effect provide for payment of loss and expense by the employer to the management contractor.

The Second Schedule of the JCT Management Contract provides for a lump sum alternative to the provision of the management contractor's services on a cost reimbursable basis. However, it envisages that adjustment of any lump sum will be by reference to a memorandum annexed to the contract (Second Schedule Part 1 Clause 3). The JCT provides no standard form of memorandum and the guidance note merely refers to the need for great care in drafting the memorandum.

Loss and expense payable to works contractors under the terms of their works contracts will generally form part of the prime cost payable to the management contractor. However, the definition of prime cost contained in the Second Schedule to the JCT Management Contract excludes 'any costs incurred as a result of any negligence by the Management Contractor in discharging his obligations under the Contract'.

JCT Works Contract/2 also distinguishes loss and expense incurred by the works contractor as a result of the actions of the employer (Clauses 4.45 and 4.46) from loss and expense incurred by the works contractor as a result of the actions of the management contractor or 'any person for whom the Management Contractor is responsible' (Clause 4.49). Clause 4.50 allows the management contractor to claim from the works contractor direct loss and expense (including the agreed claims of other works contractors) caused to the management contractor by the act, omission or default of the works contractor. As in the case of variations, loss and expense for which the employer is responsible are ascertained by the quantity surveyor (in consultation with the management contractor) under Clause 4.45. Loss and expense for which the management contractor is responsible or which are recoverable by the management contractor from the works contractor are to be agreed between the management contractor and works contractor. Failing agreement, the remedy is arbitration.

8 SET-OFF AND DEDUCTION

The provisions in works contracts which regulate set-off and deduction have developed from traditional sub-contracting forms. The JCT form of works contract, Works Contract/2, substantially adopts the provisions contained in NSC/4. The risk that one works contractor's default or delay may affect other works contract packages is inherent in the management contracting system. Difficulties are also created by the operation of the relief principle (discussed in Chapter 11).

Thus, for example, NSC/4 Clause 23.2.1 provides:

'Subject to clause 23.2.2, where the Contractor has a claim for loss and/or expense and/or damage *which he has suffered or incurred* by reason of any breach of, or failure to observe the provisions of, the Sub-Contract by the Sub-Contractor (whether or not the Contractor may have further claims for loss and/or expense and/or damage by reason of any such breach or failure) the Contractor shall be entitled to set off the amount of such loss and/or expense and/or damage *so suffered or incurred* against any money otherwise due under the Sub-Contract from the Contractor to the Sub-Contractor ...' (emphasis added).

JCT Works Contract/2 Clause 4.34 provides:

'Subject to clause 4.34.2, where the Management Contractor has a claim for loss and/or expense and/or damage by reason of any breach of, or failure to observe the provisions of, the Works Contract by the Works Contractor (whether or not the Management Contractor may have further claims for loss and/or expense and/or damage by reason of any such breach or failure) the Management Contractor shall be entitled to set off the amount of such loss and/or expense and/or damage against any money otherwise due under the Works Contract from the Contractor to the Works Contractor ...'.

It is immediately apparent that the efficacy of the set-off provisions in JCT Works Contract/2 depends on the efficacy of the devices used in the Management Contract to prevent the works contractor raising the 'no loss' argument.

Under NSC/4, no set-off which relates to any delay in completion by the sub-contractor may be made under Clause 23.2 unless the architect has certified the sub-contractor's failure to complete on time. The requirement under JCT Works Contract/2 is that the management contractor should have responded to the works contractor's notices of delay and has also himself notified the works contractor of the works contractor's failure to complete on time. There must be a question as to the effect of this provision in the light of the decision of the Court of Appeal in the two cases of *Rosehaugh Stanhope (Broadgate Phase 6) Plc and Rosehaugh Stanhope (Broadgate Phase 7) Plc v Redpath Dorman Long Ltd* (1990) and *Beaufort House Development Ltd v Zimmcor (International) Inc, and others* (1990).

CHAPTER 7

TIME OBLIGATIONS

1 EMPLOYER'S TIME-RELATED OBLIGATIONS

As under a traditional main contract, the employer must give the management contractor possession of the site so that work can begin. For example, Clause 2.3.1 of the JCT Management Contract requires the employer to let the management contractor have possession of the site if the employer gives notice to proceed under Clause 2.1.

Under the JCT documentation, the duty to give possession is a strict obligation and arises as soon as notice is given to proceed. However, Clause 2.3.2 of the JCT Management Contract enables the employer to defer possession for up to six weeks. This clause applies only if the Appendix: Part 1 so states. The deferment provision protects the employer from the consequences of a failure to give possession, such as the loss of his right to rely on the liquidated damages clause or even the possibility that the management contractor may treat the contract as terminated because of the breach. If the employer defers giving possession, the management contractor may be entitled to an extension of time. In JCT terminology, the deferment is a 'project extension item' under Clause 2.13 of the JCT Management Contract.

The employer also specifies the contract completion date, although this will be agreed in consultation with the management contractor and the professional team. In the JCT 87 documents, the date should be inserted in the Appendix: Part 2 of the Management Contract before the construction period begins. If no date for completion is inserted in the Appendix: Part 2, it is likely that an agreement to complete within a reasonable time will be implied.

A failure by the employer to comply with some of his other obligations will lead to delay, so these obligations may also be thought of as time-related. Examples include the obligation to cause drawings, specification and cost plan to be prepared (Article 6 of the JCT Management Contract) and to cause such drawings, specifications and bills of quantities for the works contracts to be prepared as are necessary (and in such a way as is necessary) to enable the management contractor to discharge his obligations properly (Article 7).

Under JCT Works Contract/2, the works contractor can claim reimbursement of loss and expense suffered because the regular progress of the works is being materially affected by any of those acts of the employer and his agents specified in Clauses 4.45 and 4.46. These defaults include deferment by the employer in giving possession of the site to the management contractor; failure of the professional team to give the management contractor (or the works contractor through the management contractor) instructions, drawings and so forth in good time; and failure of the employer to make available in good time means of access to or from the site. These provisions mean that the works contractor can obtain payment on certificate as the works progress. This right to claim loss and expense is not dependent on a right to claim an extension of time.

2 ARCHITECT'S TIME-RELATED OBLIGATIONS

Under the JCT 87 documentation, the architect's formal role is restricted mainly to the management contract, although in practice he will probably have a strong influence on the way that the management contractor performs parallel functions under the works contracts. Management contracts generally, like traditional main contracts, give the architect an important role to play in connection with extensions of time, acceleration orders and liquidated damages, all of which are discussed later in this chapter.

In addition, the architect provides the management contractor with contract documents and drawings. The late provision of these will delay the management contractor's performance of his work (for example, see Clauses 1.9 and 1.10 of the JCT Management Contract). The management contractor – like a traditional main contractor – will be entitled to claim any extra cost which he would not have incurred but for the delay. If the late provision of information means that the management contractor cannot complete on time, he will not be liable to the employer for late completion, since the employer cannot take advantage of his own wrong.

3 MANAGEMENT CONTRACTOR'S TIME-RELATED OBLIGATIONS UNDER THE MANAGEMENT CONTRACT

The traditional main contractor is responsible for completion on time (subject to extensions of time) and the payment of liquidated and ascertained damages for late completion. Management contractors have similar duties. Article 1 of the JCT Management Contract is typical in that it obliges the management contractor to 'secure' the completion of the project on or before the completion date. Clause 2.3.1 provides that completion on time must be 'ensured'.

The use of the words 'secure' and 'ensure' suggests a guarantee, onerous personal liability and severe consequences in case of failure to comply. However, the risk limitation which is an essential part of the management contract means that, even if the management contractor is theoretically liable for liquidated damages, relief provisions such as those in Clause 3.21 of the JCT Management Contract (discussed in Chapter 11) will protect him. Even so, in the light of the strong language used to impose duties on the management contractor, he may find it difficult to establish that blame lies entirely with the works contractors.

If the management contractor fails to programme and organise the work properly and the employer suffers loss, the employer will have a right of action against the management contractor for breach of contract. In negotiations, a management contractor might try to amend the contract to allow an argument that he is not liable even where a loss appears to have been caused by his own default. In the USA, construction managers have tried to escape liability for poor programming by including 'no damages for delay' clauses.

The management contractor's basic underlying duty, expressed, for example, in Article 1.1 and Clause 1.4 of the JCT Management Contract, is to co-operate with the professional team. This positive duty means among other things that he must bring to the attention of the professional team the possibility of an earlier completion date and chase the team for the additional information needed to bring about that earlier completion.

Pre-construction phase

During the pre-construction phase, the management contractor's obligations are advisory and preparatory. Article 1.1 of the JCT Management Contract requires the management contractor to co-operate with the professional team during the design stages and in planning, programming and cost estimating. Clause 1.5, which lists the general obligations of the management contractor, requires him to prepare the necessary programmes (Clause 1.5.1).

The Third Schedule of the JCT Management Contract sets out specific items for which the management contractor is responsible. Similar obligations are likely to occur in most forms of management contract. Although all these items can be performed at either the pre-construction or construction stage, the first 15 items in the Third Schedule are services that the management contractor must perform primarily during the pre-construction period.

The time-related obligations of a management contractor at the pre-construction stage are generally to help the professional team draw up an overall programme, to highlight critical items of work, to break the work into suitable packages and to indicate the design and procurement programmes necessary to allow works contractors to be appointed in good time (thus ensuring compliance with the overall programme). The management contractor's programming and construction skills should ensure that the work is arranged so as to proceed in a quick and orderly way.

Construction phase

The management contractor's obligations during the construction period are likely to be along the lines of those stated generally in Article 1 of the Articles to the JCT Management Contract. He must co-operate with the professional team in securing the carrying out and completion of the project. He must also 'set out, manage, organise, supervise and secure the carrying out and completion of the Project on or before the Date of Completion or such other date as may be fixed under the Conditions'.

Clause 2.3.1 of the JCT Management Contract restates these general obligations. It provides that, on gaining possession of the site, the management contractor 'shall secure the commencement of the Project and shall ensure the regular and diligent progress of the Project and its completion on or before the Completion Date'. Clause 3.21.1.2 states that, in the event of works contractor breach, the management contractor shall take all necessary steps 'to secure the satisfactory completion of the Project'.

Clause 1.5 gives seven general duties, some of which are time-related duties or duties with timing consequences. The JCT Third Schedule lists more specific items, including some time-related provisions (which are likely to be similar in other management contracts).

In summary, the management contractor's more important time-related obligations during construction are generally to supervise, organise and manage the project; to prepare and maintain the necessary programmes; to enter into works contracts in good time to permit completion; to co-ordinate and monitor the various works packages, making sure that works contractors are aware of the detailed construction programme; and to ensure the project is carried out by the works contractors in an expeditious way.

One of the main duties of the management contractor is to act as the project's programming expert. In theory, once his programme has been agreed at the start, all activities must be timed to comply with it. The programme will co-ordinate all the works to be carried out by works contractors. The overall project programme is made up of various separate but interfacing programmes. There will be a programme for the erection of the building; a procurement programme which deals with allocation of work into works packages and which is a composite of the programmes for each works package; and a design programme which will show the design team when design information must be available.

Employer's remedies

If the employer can establish breach of contract by the management contractor, he can claim damages. He may, however, find it hard to prove breach of certain imprecise duties, such as the duty to 'ensure the regular and diligent progress of the Project' found in Clause 2.3.1 of the JCT Management Contract.

Alternatively, the architect can decline to certify items. This is possible, for example, under the Second Schedule of the JCT Management Contract, which sets out provisions as to prime cost. The Second Schedule contains an overriding exclusion of any costs incurred because the management contractor has been negligent in discharging his contractual obligations. Such costs are simply not part of the prime cost at all.

Under the JCT Management Contract, if the management contractor refuses to agree a reasonable date for completion, so that the Appendix: Part 2 cannot be signed and dated, the employer is unlikely to have any redress for losses such as money spent employing another management contractor, because 'agreements to agree' are not enforceable in English law (as discussed in Chapter 5, Section 1).

4 MANAGEMENT CONTRACTOR'S TIME-RELATED OBLIGATIONS UNDER THE WORKS CONTRACT

The management contractor must keep the works contractor informed of progress on the project as a whole, so that the works contractor can comply with his obligation to complete the works reasonably in accordance with progress on the project. In the JCT 87 documentation, the works contractor's obligation is found in Clause 2.1 of JCT Works Contract/2, the works contract conditions.

It is the management contractor who awards extensions of time under the works contract (see Section 6). However, it is the architect who decides whether practical completion of the works contract works has been achieved. The management contractor merely certifies practical completion in accordance with the architect's decision. The management contractor also has various duties in the context of acceleration under the works contract (see Section 8).

Clause 3.1 of JCT Works Contract/2 obliges the management contractor to issue the drawings, instructions and other information which the works contractor needs to complete the works in accordance with the works contract. This is in addition to the information already included in the works contract.

The works contractor can claim for loss and expense arising from disturbance of the regular progress of the works caused by an act or default of the management contractor or his agents (JCT Works Contract/2 Clause 4.49).

Under Clause 7.6 of JCT Works Contract/2, the works contractor may determine his employment on various grounds, one of which is that the management contractor without reasonable cause fails to proceed with securing the carrying out and completion of the project so that the reasonable progress of the works is seriously affected. The right to determine arises only if a remedy under any other provisions of the works contract will not adequately recompense the works contractor. In most cases the payment of loss and expense will probably be adequate recompense.

5 WORKS CONTRACTOR'S TIME-RELATED OBLIGATIONS

It is generally true that the works contractor's obligations - including his time-related obligations - increase under the management contracting system. For example, a works contractor may have to accelerate the works without financial recompense and programme his part of the works to accord with the progress of other trades.

The works contract

Clause 1.6.1 of JCT Works Contract/2 provides that the works contractor's liability to the management contractor for breach of the terms of the works contract includes liability incurred by the management contractor to the employer for breaches of the management contract arising out of the works contractor's default. This would include, for example, the management contractor's liability to pay liquidated damages.

Clause 2.1 of JCT Works Contract/2 requires the works contractor to carry out and complete the works in accordance with the details in Item 1 of the tender, which specifies periods required for submission of the works contractor's drawings and for the execution of the works. The works contractor's timing obligations are subject to the progress of the project as a whole and to the grant of extensions of time. The management contractor must keep the works contractor sufficiently informed about progress of the project for the works contractor to comply with his obligations. Under Clause 7.1, failure by the works contractor to proceed with the works in the manner provided in Clause 2.1 is a default which may lead to determination of the works contractor's employment.

The works contractor is required by Clause 2.2 of JCT Works Contract/2 to give notice of any delay to the management contractor. (This is considered further in the context of extensions of time in Section 6 below.) The works contractor must use his best endeavours to prevent delay and to do all that is reasonably required to the satisfaction of the management contractor to proceed with the works (Clause 2.8).

Clause 4.50 of JCT Works Contract/2 allows the management contractor to claim for loss and expense suffered as a result of disturbance of the regular progress of the works arising from acts or defaults of the works contractor or his agents. This provision reflects Clauses 4.45 to 4.46 and 4.49, which allow the works contractor to claim for loss and expense arising from defaults of the employer and management contractor.

Direct agreement between employer and works contractor

If the employer wishes to be able to bring a direct action against the works contractor, rather than relying on indirect enforcement through the management contractor, he must enter into a separate agreement with the works contractor. The JCT 87 documentation includes Works Contract/3, a direct agreement between employer and works contractor. However, the collateral warranty in that agreement is limited, since it applies only to works contractors with a design responsibility.

Clause 2 of JCT Works Contract/3 requires the works contractor to supply the architect with information (including drawings) in accordance with any agreed programme or at such time as the architect may reasonably require, so that the architect will not be delayed in issuing necessary instructions or drawings to the management contractor. There is no equivalent obligation in JCT Works Contract/2, which leads to an anomalous situation. It would be helpful if the works contractor's duties to supply information were also owed to the management contractor, who may manage the design insofar as it is carried out by works contractors.

The employer may wish to seek warranties beyond those in JCT Works Contract/3. For example, the employer will benefit from a warranty that the works contractor should perform so that he does not cause delay to the project. Under the JCT documentation, the employer has no direct remedy for slow progress on site.

6 EXTENSIONS OF TIME

Any management contract will usually include an extension of time clause. There will also be provision for extending the completion date of the works contractor's package. As in any construction contract, the extension of time clause protects both employer and contractor. The management contractor avoids a possible liability to pay liquidated and ascertained damages, while the employer is reassured by the knowledge that his right to claim liquidated damages in the future is preserved and operates from the extended date.

Extensions of time under the management contract

The extension of time provisions in the JCT Management Contract are found in Clauses 2.12 to 2.14. Under Clause 2.12, the management contractor is required to advise the architect at once when it becomes apparent that any cause of delay (not just one entitling him to an extension of time) is likely to put off the completion date. It is not entirely clear to whom it must be 'reasonably apparent' that the works will not be completed by the due date – suggestions have variously been made that the relevant party is the management contractor, or the employer, or the professional team.

Under the JCT Management Contract (as under JCT 80), the architect grants the extension. The architect has a duty to grant a fair and reasonable extension of time if, on considering the management contractor's application, he forms the opinion that the project is likely to be or has been delayed by a 'project extension item'. The architect is to give the extension of time as soon as he is able; there is no set time limit.

Clause 2.12 provides that no extension shall be made if the delay is one which the management contractor has not used his best endeavours to avoid or reduce. The proviso at the end of Clause 2.13, to the effect that no project extension item shall be considered if caused by default of the management contractor, emphasises this. If the management contractor is in breach of contract, he will be unable to claim the protection of Clause 3.21 and the relieving provisions, and will be liable to pay liquidated and ascertained damages as a result of the delay.

Grounds of entitlement

The grounds of entitlement to an extension of time will be specified in the management contract. They will usually include defaults or delays by the employer or design team and the entitlement of a works contractor to an extension of time under the works contract. However, not every works contract delay results in a project delay.

Clause 2.13 of the JCT Management Contract lists 'project extension items' which give rise to entitlement to an extension. Clause 2.13 also contains a proviso that no project extension item is to be considered to the extent that it was caused or contributed to by any default of the management contractor, his servants, or agents, or any works contractor or his servants, agents or sub-contractors. Project extension items are:

- any cause which impedes proper discharge by the management contractor of his obligations under the management contract. Three examples are listed (it should be stressed that they are no more than examples). These are default by the employer or any person for whom he is responsible; failure to provide the management contractor in due time with all necessary specifications, instructions and drawings which have been applied for at reasonable times; and deferment of giving the management contractor possession of the site under Clause 2.3.1 (provided that Clause 2.3.2, the deferment provision, has been included); and

- any 'relevant event' which causes delay to the completion date. Relevant events are those entitling any works contractor to an extension of time under Clause 2.3 or Clause 2.7 of JCT Works Contract/2.

One relevant event is specifically stated not to be a ground for extension under the management contract – that is, delay on the part of works contractors (Clause 2.10.7.1 of JCT Works Contract/2). This reflects the second part of the proviso in Clause 2.13 of the JCT Management Contract, excluding project extension items caused by works contractor default. In deciding whether to grant an extension of time to the management contractor, the architect must therefore also be aware of the operation of all the works contracts.

There will be no extension of time under the JCT Management Contract if a works contractor is late because of a delay by a preceding works contractor or by his own default. (The innocent works contractor will be entitled to an extension of time under his works contract.) The management contractor will be in breach of contract, although still protected by the relieving provisions in Clause 3.21. The management contractor will have to pursue the defaulting works contractor for the liquidated damages to which the employer is entitled, as well as any other additional costs which the management contractor has incurred, including the claims of innocent works contractors.

Clause 2.10 of JCT Works Contract/2 lists 13 relevant events. These include force majeure; adverse weather; civil commotion and strike; the management contractor or the works contractor through the management contractor not having received in due time instructions, drawings, and information; delay by other works contractors or nominated suppliers which the management contractor has taken all practicable steps to avoid; the works contractor's unforeseeable inability to secure essential labour, goods or materials; the failure of the employer to give access to and from the site in due time; and deferment in giving possession of the site to the management contractor (if Clause 2.3.2 of the JCT Management Contract applies).

Power to fix an earlier completion date

This power is set out in Clause 2.12.2 of the JCT Management Contract and is exercisable by the architect. It cannot be exercised until after the first award of an extension of time, and then only if an omission instructed after that award justifies the earlier date. The new date is to be earlier than the date previously fixed under the extension of time provisions. A similar provision in Clause 2.6 of JCT Works Contract/2 is exercisable by the management contractor.

Extensions of time under the works contract

If it becomes reasonably apparent that the commencement, progress or completion of the works is likely to be delayed, the works contractor is to give written notice to the management contractor of the material circumstances, including the cause of delay (Clause 2.2.1 of JCT Works Contract/2). Under Clause 2.3.1, the management contractor has the duty to give an extension of time to the works contractor if:

- the works contractor submits the relevant notice, particulars and estimate in accordance with the contract;
- the management contractor believes any of the causes of delay to be a relevant event or an act of default of the management contractor (or someone for whom the management contractor is responsible); and
- the completion of the works is likely to be delayed beyond the period specified in the works contract.

The works contractor must have used his best endeavours to prevent delay (Clause 2.8). It should be noted that relevant events include delay by another works contractor (mentioned in Clause 2.10.7), although this, as already indicated, is not a project extension item under the management contract.

If the delay results from a lawful suspension of the works by the works contractor under Clause 4.28 (because of non-payment), the delay is deemed to have been caused by default of the management contractor.

The general extension of time provisions under JCT Works Contract/2 are broadly similar to those found in the JCT 80 nominated sub-contract, except that the management contractor rather than the architect decides whether the extension of time is to be given. This difference creates the possibility of a discrepancy between extensions under the management contract and under the works contract.

The management contractor must, if reasonably practicable, fix the extension of time within 12 weeks of receipt of notice from the works contractor or before the expiry of the period for completion of the works if that is sooner (JCT Works Contract/2 Clause 2.4). He is to state on which ground the extension is based and the extent to which he has had regard to instructions issued since the previous fixing of a revised period for completion of the works (Clause 2.5).

If the date for completion of the works falls before practical completion, the management contractor must carry out a review of awards of extensions of time, having first notified the architect. The management contractor can then revise the period for completion or confirm the previous period (Clause 2.7).

Under Clause 2.14 of the JCT Management Contract, the management contractor has to keep the architect informed of proposed works contract extensions of time. He must notify the architect in sufficient time to allow the architect to dissent in writing before the management contractor is obliged to notify the works contractor (in accordance with Clauses 2.3 and 2.4 of JCT Works Contract/2) of the extension of time to be awarded. This should allow the management contractor to ensure that extensions he grants to works contractors are in accordance with extensions of time he receives under the management contract, and he will probably be protected from the risk of the architect later disagreeing with him. However, the management contractor loses this protection if the architect simply fails to give any indication at all before the management contractor is obliged to notify the works contractor of the extension of time.

The architect may dissent from the proposed extension of time and the management contractor must notify the works contractor of dissent. The consequences of dissent are not spelled out. It has been suggested that dissent acts as a bar on the management contractor granting the proposed extension. However, it seems more likely that the management contractor is free to go ahead and grant the extension, although a conflict of this sort between the architect and the management contractor is undesirable. In addition, if the management contractor has granted too long an extension of time, he may have items of prime cost disallowed. He is also likely to be at risk as to liquidated damages if he awards the works contractor a longer extension of time than he obtains from the architect under the management contract. The management contractor will not be able to recover these liquidated damages from the works contractor. Certainly, the management contractor's easiest option is to rely on the architect to decide the extension of time due to the works contractor, provided the architect is willing to do so.

7 LIQUIDATED AND ASCERTAINED DAMAGES

Damages payable by the management contractor to the employer

The procedure relating to liquidated and ascertained damages in the JCT Management Contract, and in most other management contracts, reflects that in JCT 80. If the management contractor fails to secure completion of the project by the completion date, the architect issues a certificate to that effect, entitling the employer to liquidated and ascertained damages for the period between the completion date and the date of practical completion (see Clauses 2.9 and 2.10 of the JCT Management Contract). Under Clause 2.4 the architect certifies practical completion, which terminates the management contractor's obligation to pay liquidated damages.

If an extension of time is granted after the issue of the Clause 2.9 certificate, the certificate is to be cancelled.

The amount of the liquidated and ascertained damages is to be stated in the Appendix: Part 1. In accordance with the general law on liquidated damages, the damages must be a genuine pre-estimate of loss in the event of delay, otherwise the provision may be void as a penalty. The JCT Management Contract assumes that a figure for liquidated and ascertained damages will be inserted, but a level of damages that is 'reasonable' for a large works package may be inappropriate for a smaller works contractor. The JCT Management Contract does not allow the flexibility of negotiating a different position with different works contractors without side letters and amendments to the Management Contract itself.

Under the JCT Management Contract, it is possible that the management contractor may never actually pay or allow liquidated damages to the employer, because the requirement is subject to the Clause 3.21 relieving provisions discussed in Chapter 11. The employer will recover liquidated damages from the management contractor only if he can establish that the delay has arisen as a result of the management contractor's own negligence or breach.

The management contractor is to keep an account of liquidated damages due to the employer if these are recovered from the works contractor. Clause 3.21.2.2 provides that the employer may keep an account of liquidated damages accruing due to him. If the management contractor recovers from the works contractor those damages due to the employer, he must pay them to the employer.

Under some forms of management contract, the management contractor is liable for liquidated and ascertained damages regardless of the level of recovery from the works contractor in default. However, this means reverting to the old adversarial position to be found in a traditional main contract. The management contractor may in those circumstances argue that the delay was caused by the design team producing information too late.

Damages payable under the works contract for late completion

Under the JCT 87 documentation, these damages are unliquidated. However, Clause 1.6.1 of JCT Works Contract/2 makes it clear that the works contractor's liability for breaches of the works contract extends to any liability the management contractor incurs under the management contract as a result of default by the works contractor. This provision enables responsibility for a portion of the liquidated and ascertained damages due from the management contractor to the employer to be passed on to the works contractor. However, difficulties will arise in working out what damages are in practice 'attributable' to a works contractor.

Clauses 2.11 and 2.12 of JCT Works Contract/2 provide that, if the works contractor fails to complete on time, the management contractor must notify him of this. Then, if the management contractor has dealt with all outstanding extension of time applications, the works contractor must pay or allow to the management contractor a sum equal to any direct loss or expense arising from the works contractor's failure. However, the management contractor cannot deduct this sum immediately because the deduction is subject to the adjudication provisions in Section 4 of JCT Works Contract/2.

Under Clause 2.14 of Works Contract/2, it is the architect who decides when practical completion has been achieved. The management contractor, with the architect's consent, then certifies practical completion. The clause does not suggest that the management contractor has any discretion: 'When in the opinion of the Architect Practical Completion ... is achieved the Management Contractor ... shall issue a certificate'. The architect's role here is surprising, since in other respects, such as extensions of time, the management contractor makes the decision. Architects should be aware of what will be involved in having to assume this responsibility for a large number of works contracts.

8 ACCELERATION

The JCT 87 documentation gives the employer the power to accelerate the works. Under Clause 3.6.2 of the JCT Management Contract, the employer has the power to cause the architect to issue a preliminary instruction, bringing forward the current completion date or cancelling or reducing the length of any extension of time being allowed to the management contractor. JCT Works Contract/2 contains provisions that complement those in the JCT Management Contract. It appears that the acceleration provisions in both contracts would permit a completion date earlier than the original completion date. Clause 2.9 of Works Contract/2 mentions the fixing of a period of completion shorter than that stated in the tender, which is possible only if the acceleration provisions in Clauses 3.4.2 to 3.4.7 apply.

Many commonly-used standard main contract forms (JCT 63, JCT 80, ICE 4 and ICE 5) do not provide for acceleration in the sense of bringing forward the completion date. Clause 46 of ICE 5 and Clause 46(1) of ICE 6 allow the engineer to order accelerated work only if progress appears to be too slow to enable the contractor to complete in due time – a different meaning of 'accelerate'.

Some more recent contracts contain simple acceleration provisions. Clause 46(3) of ICE 6 provides for accelerated completion in the sense of completion 'within a revised time being less than the time or extended time for completion', but only where the contractor agrees to accelerate. Any special terms or conditions of payment are to be agreed between the employer and contractor before any acceleration action is taken. Clause 46(3) gives no procedures to be followed and adds nothing to the pre-existing position, since the parties can in any event accelerate if they agree to do so. GC Works 1/Ed 3 (Clause 38) also has an acceleration provision. If the 'Authority' (the employer) wishes to achieve early completion, it will direct the contractor to submit price and timing proposals or to explain why acceleration is impossible. If the Authority accepts the contractor's proposals, it will specify the new date and consequential amendments to price and programme. The contractor may also initiate an acceleration proposal.

Acceleration can, of course, always be achieved by agreement between the parties. The JCT Management Contract acceleration provisions, like the ICE 6 and GC Works 1/Ed 3 provisions, do little more than reflect what happens in practice in any construction contract when acceleration is achieved by negotiation.

Acceleration under the JCT 87 documentation

The JCT acceleration clause is optional. Clause 3.6 of the Management Contract will apply only if the Management Contract Appendix: Part 1 says so and the Works Contract Invitation to Tender (item 5) states that Clause 3.6 of the Management Contract applies (see Clause 3.4.2 of JCT Works Contract/2).

Where the architect has issued a preliminary acceleration instruction, Clause 3.6.4 of the JCT Management Contract allows the management contractor (and through him any works contractor) to make a reasonable objection to compliance. Clause 3.4.4 of Works Contract/2 provides that the works contractor has seven days from receipt of the instruction to object in writing. He makes his objection to the management contractor, who passes the objection and his own comments to the architect. No time limit is set for the management contractor to convey the objections to the architect. If the works contractor has no objection, or if the architect considers the objection not to be reasonable, the preliminary instruction is reissued. If the objection is reasonable, the preliminary instruction is withdrawn (or varied and reissued).

Under Clause 3.4.6 of JCT Works Contract/2, the works contractor has to inform the management contractor of the lump sum that is required to accelerate (or that it is impracticable to calculate such a lump sum). He must also inform the management contractor of the timing changes that will apply. Clause 3.6.5 of the Management Contract requires the management contractor to notify the architect of the lump sum (or the fact that the lump sum cannot be stated) and of the suitable new completion date, or of the extent to which an extension of time can be avoided or reduced.

If the employer agrees to the extra payments and the proposed new completion date or reduction in extension of time, he can order the architect to issue the acceleration instruction under Clause 3.6.6 of the JCT Management Contract. The management contractor then instructs the works contractors in a similar manner under Clause 3.4.7 of JCT

Works Contract/2. The acceleration takes effect and the management contractor receives the relevant payments.

Clause 3.4.7 of JCT Works Contract/2 provides that if the management contractor issues instructions for expedition, confirming the works contractor's proposals made under Clause 3.4.6 (as to payment required and changes to programme), the works contractor shall comply with the earlier completion date or cancellation or reduction of the extension of time ordered.

The acceleration provisions in the JCT 87 documents attempt to balance the employer's need for flexibility against the works contractor's need to be compensated financially. This procedure tries to be fair to all parties, but it is extremely cumbersome. Another criticism is that the seven days allowed for the works contractor to object is very short. In addition, the meaning of a 'reasonable' objection is open to dispute. It seems that the architect can simply ignore an objection as 'unreasonable', although in practice it may be unlikely that an acceleration would take place if the management contractor or works contractor did object.

As has already been mentioned, Clause 2.12.2 of the JCT Management Contract gives the architect (and Clause 2.6 of JCT Works Contract/2 gives the management contractor) the power to fix a completion date earlier than one previously fixed as a result of an extension of time. The power arises if it is fair and reasonable to alter the date, having regard to the omission of work or obligations since the time of that previous extension.

CHAPTER 8

QUALITY OBLIGATIONS

This chapter discusses the contractual responsibilities of the various parties for the quality of construction. However, it should be remembered that obligations in this area may also arise in tort. For example, if loss and damage are suffered as a result of faulty design or workmanship, the designer or builder may be liable in negligence (subject to the present reluctance of the courts to allow claims for economic loss alone).

European Community legislation

The requirements of European Community law should also be considered, particularly in relation to the quality of 'products'. For example, the EC directive on product liability, implemented by Part I of the Consumer Protection Act 1987, imposes strict liability for certain damage arising from defects in products. (Damage must consist of death, personal injury, or damage to an item or property other than the defective product itself.) It is not entirely clear whether a building itself, as well as the materials used in its construction, would be 'products' under the Act; the directive defines 'product' as a movable, even if incorporated into an immovable.

The Construction Products Regulations 1991 implement another EC directive on products. The Regulations extend to all products produced for incorporation in a permanent manner in construction works (other than 'minor products'). The aim is to see that products have the characteristics necessary to enable the construction works as a whole to satisfy essential requirements such as stability, safety in use and fire safety. If a product complies with the appropriate standards and technical specification, the 'CE' mark can be affixed.

1 MANAGEMENT CONTRACTOR'S OBLIGATIONS

Limitations on obligations

The traditional main contractor's duties include responsibility for the performance and quality of the main contract works and all sub-contract works. This is not the case for most management contractors because, under a management contract, it is the works contractors who are responsible for completion of the works and the employer who bears the ultimate financial risk (in accordance with, for example, Clause 3.21 of the JCT Management Contract).

Clause 1.5.3 of the JCT Management Contract requires the management contractor to ensure that the works contractor completes all the work in the works package, in accordance with the project specification and the works contracts and in compliance with the requirements for standards of materials and workmanship. In accordance with Clause 3.21.1, the management contractor must therefore ensure that defects are remedied by the works contractor and must pursue the works contractor for damages resulting from the defect. Beyond that, the management contractor is not liable for any defects in workmanship and materials unless he has been negligent in performing his own duties of management and supervision and (where appropriate) design.

The management contractor's duties

Some of the management contractor's quality-related duties, such as that to inspect the quality of the works, overlap with duties of the architect. Others overlap with the duties of the works contractor (such as the duty to see that design drawings are produced on time).

The management contractor is responsible for programming and may also have certain design duties. (His design duties were discussed in Chapter 6, Section 2.) However, most of the management contractor's quality-related activities are supervisory: essentially, he must supervise and manage the project so that the end result is a structure whose workmanship and materials are of an appropriate standard. In considering whether the management contractor has done his job properly it is therefore necessary to consider what standards the workmanship and materials produced by the works contractors must meet as well as what standard of supervisory, managerial, programming and design skill is required of the management contractor.

Management and supervision

A management contractor is likely to be under a duty to ensure that work done by the works contractors is carried out in accordance with the project specification and in accordance with the works contracts, using materials, goods and workmanship of the specified quality and standards – for example, a duty of this sort is found in Clause 1.5.3 of the JCT Management Contract. Clause 1.5.3 goes on to provide that the management contractor must ensure that, where and to the extent that approval of quality of materials or standards of workmanship is a matter for the opinion of the architect, that quality and those standards are to the reasonable satisfaction of the architect.

The project specification should set out the applicable standards clearly, to avoid uncertainty, and the standards in the works contract should be consistent with those in the project specification. If there is a conflict between the project specification and the works contract, it could be argued that the higher standard should prevail, since the employer can insist on both criteria.

Qualities and standards are often expressed by reference to an objective measure, such as British Standards or a Code of Practice. Sometimes, the architect's reasonable satisfaction is the criterion, in which case his inspection duties will be particularly onerous. Clause 1.14.1.1 of the JCT Management Contract and Clause 4.32.1.1 of JCT Works Contract/2 provide that the final certificate is to be conclusive evidence that the quality of materials or standard of workmanship are to the satisfaction of the architect (in those cases where the quality or standard were required to be to his satisfaction). The employer's remedies against the management contractor will therefore cease once the period for challenging the final certificate by arbitration expires. The employer is then left only with a remedy against the architect, based on negligent inspection.

Clause 1.5.5 of the JCT Management Contract requires the management contractor to provide continual supervision and to perform and provide everything necessary for the organisation and management of the project.

Clause 2.5 of the JCT Management Contract requires the architect to specify in a schedule of defects any defects which appear during the defects liability period and which are due to materials, goods or workmanship not being in accordance with the contract. Subject to Clause 3.21, the management contractor is to 'secure' the making good of defects at no expense to the employer. The works contractor, not the management contractor, will carry out the actual repair works. The reference to Clause 3.21 is a reminder that the employer will ultimately bear the financial risk, including the risk of a defaulting works contractor failing to rectify a defect.

Clauses 3.8 to 3.12 of the JCT Management Contract deal specifically with materials, goods and workmanship. Similar provisions are found in Clause 1.7 of JCT Works Contract/2 - see Section 2 of this chapter.

Clause 3.8.1 amplifies the provisions of Clause 1.5.3, requiring materials and goods to be of the kinds and standards described in the project specification or in the bill of quantities or specification of any works contract, so far as they are procurable. Similarly, Clause 3.8.2 requires workmanship to be of the standards in the project specification, or the bill of quantities or specification of any works contract, or (if no such standards are described) to a standard appropriate to the project. There is an absolute obligation to provide workmanship of the relevant standard, and it is no excuse that skilled labour is in short supply, and so not 'procurable'. Where the project specification so provides, or where it is otherwise so provided, materials, goods and workmanship are to be to the reasonable satisfaction of the architect.

Clause 3.11 requires the management contractor to comply with the architect's instructions for the removal from the site of any work, materials or goods which are not in accordance with the contract, at no cost to the employer. Again, though, this is expressly subject to Clause 3.21.

Clause 3.12 requires the management contractor to comply or secure compliance with the architect's instructions requiring any defect, shrinkage or other fault which appears or is discovered and which is due to materials, goods or workmanship not in accordance with the contract, to be made good at no cost to the employer, subject to Clause 3.21. This applies to defects discovered at any time.

Clause 3.21.1.2 requires the management contractor to secure satisfactory completion of the works after works contractor breach.

The Third Schedule to the JCT Management Contract includes several specific quality-related services to be performed by the management contractor. For example, he must make regular visits to the workplaces of works contractors and suppliers to inspect, among other things, quality (paragraph 21). He must supervise the production of all site work and ensure the necessary quality and prompt replacement of defective work in accordance with works contracts (paragraph 43). He must also see that works contractors make good any damage to the work of other works contractors and remedy defects after practical completion of their works (paragraphs 44 to 45). Furthermore, he is to 'secure the prompt remedying' of defects listed by the architect after practical completion of the project and at the end of the defects liability period (paragraph 46).

It is thus apparent that the management contractor must set up an effective quality control system and supervise the progress of the works. Where he fails to do this, and the quality of the work suffers, he will be directly liable to the employer. The management contractor must also make sure that all damage and defects are corrected by the works contractor, who may levy contra-charges on other works contractors when necessary. If a works contractor is in default and walks off site, the management contractor will appoint another works contractor to remedy the defect and complete the works. Payment will be the responsibility of the employer, subject to successful claims against the defaulting works contractor.

2 WORKS CONTRACTOR'S OBLIGATIONS

Because the management contractor avoids many of the usual functions of a main contractor in a traditional construction contract, the works contractor will usually take on the burden of additional onerous conditions and problems. Each works contractor has complete responsibility for the work in his package.

Standard of care

A works contract will probably specify the level of skill to be used by the works contractor, and the standard the materials must satisfy. Clause 1.7 of JCT Works Contract/2 and Article 1 of JCT Works Contract/3 set out the standards applicable to the works contract works.

Under Clause 1.7.2 of JCT Works Contract/2, the works contractor is to provide materials and goods, so far as procurable, of the kinds and standards described in the works contract (or to the reasonable satisfaction of the architect where that is the criterion). Under Clause 1.7.3, the works contractor is to provide workmanship of the standard described in the works contract or appropriate to the works if no standard is described (or, again, to the reasonable satisfaction of the architect where that is the criterion). Similar provisions are found in Clause 3.8.1 and 3.8.2 of the JCT Management Contract. Clause 4.32.1.1 of JCT Works Contract/2 provides that the final certificate is conclusive evidence that works are to the satisfaction of the architect.

The provisions as to standards of materials and workmanship are similar to those found in traditional sub-contracts. In addition, Clause 1.7.4 of JCT Works Contract/2 includes a design obligation, which is more usually found in direct agreements between employers and sub-contractors. The management contractor is liable to the employer for all breaches by the works contractor, including design breaches, so it makes sense for the works contractor to be liable to the management contractor in turn. Clause 1.7.4 is very similar to the warranty found in Works Contract/3 (the employer/works contractor agreement).

Under Clause 1.7.4 of JCT Works Contract/2 (and Article 1 of JCT Works Contract/3), the works contractor is to exercise all reasonable skill and care:

- in design, insofar as he designs the works;
- in the selection of materials and goods, insofar as he selects them; and
- in the satisfaction of any performance specification or requirement, insofar as it is included or referred to in the works contract.

Possible difficulties of interpretation arise from the different standards specified in Clause 1.7.2 and 1.7.3 (compliance with the contract) and in Clause 1.7.4 (reasonable skill and care), when both standards apply to a specific item of work.

The provisions (in Clause 1.7.2 and 1.7.3 of JCT Works Contract/2 and Clause 3.8.1 and 3.8.2 of the JCT Management Contract) that goods and workmanship must meet the standards specified in the contract are somewhat contradicted by the provisions in Clause 1.7.4.2 and 1.7.4.3 of JCT Works Contract/2 (also to be found in Article 1 of Works Contract/3), which state that only reasonable skill and care need be exercised in the selection of materials and goods, and in satisfying any performance specification or contractual requirement. If the specification or bills lay down a standard that is higher than can be achieved by exercising reasonable skill and care in selection of goods, it is arguable that the lower standard applies, since Clause 1.4 states that terms in the conditions override those in the bills or specification.

Other obligations in the works contract

Clause 3.4.1.2 of JCT Works Contract/2 provides an exception to the usual rule that the works contractor 'shall forthwith comply' with an instruction of the architect or direction of the management contractor. Where the instruction or direction alters any part of the works to which Clause 1.7.4 refers, the written consent of the works contractor is necessary. His consent cannot be unreasonably withheld.

Clause 1.10.3 provides that the quality (and quantity) of the work included in the works contract sum or tender sum shall be deemed to be that set out in the bills of quantity. This work would include design work carried out by the works contractor, since payment for it is included in the works contract sum. Since the bills of quantity are among the numbered documents, all other documents forming the works contract take precedence if there is a conflict (Clause 1.4). It may be that the bills will specify a higher standard than the 'reasonable skill and care' required by Clause 1.7.4, and that the bills will be overruled.

Under Clause 2.15, the works contractor is liable for defects in the works occurring before practical completion of the works and arising, inter alia, from materials or workmanship not being in accordance with works contract standards. This provision does not seem to extend to design defects, although such an extension would make sense. It is not clear who is liable for damage occurring between practical completion of the works, and the start of the defects liability period (which is likely to be the same as the defects liability period for the project as a whole), but it is probably the management contractor.

Clause 7.1.3 lists as grounds for determination by the management contractor of the works contractor's employment a refusal (after written notice) to remove defective work or improper materials and goods, so that the project is materially affected, and a failure to rectify defects where the works contractor is required to rectify them.

Direct employer/works contractor agreement

There will often be a direct warranty agreement between the employer and at least some of the works contractors, which may contain onerous collateral warranty conditions. In the JCT 87 documentation, Works Contract/3 is an optional agreement between the employer and the works contractor.

JCT Works Contract/3 contains a warranty by the works contractor to exercise reasonable skill and care in design and in selection of materials and goods, and in satisfaction of any performance specification in the sub-contract documents. The warranty is very similar to that in NSC/2 and to Clause 1.7.4 of the JCT Management Contract.

Even if reasonable skill and care are exercised, the end result may fall short of the specification. This warranty therefore affords the employer less protection than a simple promise to comply with the specification. Many employers try to impose on the designer an absolute warranty as to compliance with the performance specification. Arguments have been advanced that the works contractor's warranty should be to design a construction that will be 'fit for purpose' rather than simply using reasonable skill and care in the design.

3 ARCHITECT'S OBLIGATIONS

The architect has certain obligations and powers under the JCT Management Contract. His basic power is to issue 'such Instructions as are reasonably necessary to enable the Management Contractor properly to discharge his functions' (Clause 3.3.1). Under Clause 3.12, the architect has the power to issue instructions requiring any defect, shrinkage or other fault appearing or discovered at any time to be made good, whenever he considers it necessary and if the defect is due to materials, goods or workmanship not being in accordance with the contract. Under Clause 2.5 to 2.6, the architect is to deliver a schedule of defects during the defects liability period and to certify the making good of defects.

The architect is not relieved of his obligations just because the management contractor has obligations to supervise site work and ensure quality control. Under the RIBA architect's appointment, Clause 3.10, the architect has a duty to inspect the progress and quality of the works and to see that they are being executed 'generally in accordance with the contract documents', although he is not required to make frequent or constant inspections. The employer may have a remedy against the architect if the latter has failed to detect bad workmanship that should have been apparent at such inspections.

As has already been mentioned, if the architect's satisfaction with standards of materials and workmanship is the applicable criterion, the final certificate is conclusive evidence of that satisfaction (JCT Management Contract, Clause 1.14.1.1). The architect's inspection duties will be more onerous in such a case.

Under Clause 8.3 of JCT Works Contract/2, unless the architect, management contractor and works contractor agree otherwise, the architect shall only nominate as supplier a person who will execute in favour of the employer a warranty in an agreed form against default in design and selection of materials, and who will enter into a contract of sale with the works contractor providing that material or goods supplied are of the specified standards, and that the supplier will make good defects in the material or goods.

CHAPTER 9

PRICING AND PAYMENT

1 PRIME COST

The factors taken into consideration when deciding whether to use a form of management contract are similar to those that the Construction Industry Research and Information Association (CIRIA) suggests favour the use of some form of cost reimbursement contract (see CIRIA Report R85 on target and cost reimbursement construction contracts).

The prime cost payable under a management contract consists of the costs actually incurred by a management contractor in carrying out the work. Management, overheads and profit are usually paid to him separately by means of a fee or fees. It may also be possible for some of the resources provided by the management contractor to be paid for by means of an agreed lump sum if the requirements for those resources can be sufficiently well defined before construction begins. (Such resources are referred to in this chapter as management contractor's preliminaries.)

It is important to remember in operating any prime cost contract that the employer and the quantity surveyor must have access to the contractor's records and accounts so that they can check the management contractor's applications for payment.

Because of the division of amounts payable under the management contract into such categories as the prime cost, fee and lump sum for management contractor's preliminaries, it is important that there is a clear definition in the management contract to show exactly what each is.

A prime cost definition is included in the JCT Management Contract as the Second Schedule. The general definition in Part 1 of the Schedule is amplified by the more detailed definition of its principal constituent parts in Parts 2 to 4C. In this, as in many management contracts, the principal categories of items which are paid for by prime cost are:

- works contracts;
- on-site staff and labour;
- materials and goods;
- plant, consumable stores and services; and (possibly)
- sundry (or miscellaneous) costs.

Works contracts

The works contracts comprise (for the purposes of prime cost) the sums payable by the management contractor to the works contractors under the terms of the works contracts. The prices of the works contract packages make up the bulk of the prime cost.

Obviously not all sums payable should be chargeable through the prime cost mechanism to the employer. For instance, sums incurred through the management contractor's default should not be reimbursable in any circumstances, and amounts due by reason of the defaults of other works contractors should be contra-charged to the works contractors involved. Definitions of prime cost will typically be drafted so that any discounts available to the management contractor under the works contracts are passed through to the employer.

On-site staff and labour

The management contractor will supply either full or part-time on-site management staff to manage the works on a day to day basis. He may also supply labourers to help with the control of the site (by providing site clearance, for instance, or distribution of materials on site) or to carry out temporary works which generally benefit the site. The cost of both these categories of manpower are sometimes included as a prime cost item. There should be some control over the costs incurred under the heading of on-site labour and the following items therefore need to be considered:

- the numbers, types and grades of persons to be engaged on the works;
- salaries and wages:
  - are these payable to agency staff?
  - are these to be limited to agreed pay scales?
- overtime and bonus payments;
- redundancy and severance pay;
- removal and disturbance allowances;
- payment of travelling fares;
- National Insurance contributions;
- contributions to pensions, life assurance, and medical schemes;
- training levies and contributions;
- expenses and allowances including any car allowances; and
- holiday pay.

Some of these items may be included in the prime cost. However, employers will not wish to reimburse all such costs and are therefore likely to require that some of these items either form part of the preliminary items or are included as part of the fee. Off-site staff costs are often included as an item of overhead in the fee.

Goods and materials

If the management contractor is supplying goods or materials directly (ie not through a works contractor or supplier) they are likely to be included as prime cost items. Again, provision is usually made for the benefit of discounts to flow through to the employer, so that the reimbursable amount is the net cost of the materials. The following factors need to be considered:

- measures to ensure that goods and materials are purchased on terms and at prices beneficial to the employer;
- provision for specifying the method of valuation of items drawn from the management contractor's own stocks;
- measures to ensure that any surpluses revert to the management contractor and are credited to the prime cost; and
- provisions for returnable packaging to ensure that any credit received for the packaging is reflected by a credit to the prime cost.

Plant, consumable stores and services

The nature of plant, stores and services whose costs are to be reimbursable as prime cost should be tightly defined in the management contract.

Plant may either be the management contractor's own plant, in which case rates for its use should be agreed, or it may be hired by him from others, in which case it will be necessary to ensure that the hire rates and terms are beneficial, with the employer receiving the benefit of any discount. Employers will also want to ensure that only necessary plant is hired and that it is hired only for as long as it is needed. Terms may be included to ensure that the presence of all plant on site is controlled and records should be kept for this purpose. Some forms of management contract specify that all plant is the responsibility of the management contractor so that he bears the risk of care of the plant, breakdowns and so forth. Consideration also needs to be given as to whether transportation costs and loading and offloading costs for the carriage of plant, materials and equipment are reimbursable as prime cost or whether they are to form part of the preliminary items or be included in the fee.

Consumable stores need to be closely monitored to guard against excessive wastage. Some forms of management contract exclude from the prime cost the cost of items where the degree of wastage, damage or loss exceeds what is reasonable.

Services need to be defined by reference to the site and the works. The cost of some items may be split (eg the first two copies of any one document may be included in the fee, with the cost of further copies being reimbursable as prime cost). The employer may place a limitation upon a particular service so that costs in respect of that service can only be incurred with his prior consent.

Sundry costs

The JCT Management Contract contains in the definition of prime cost in the Second Schedule a list of 'sundry' items. In other forms of management contract, these items are often found in the list of items designated as 'plant, consumable stores or services' or even form part of the management contractor's preliminaries.

2 MANAGEMENT CONTRACTOR'S PRELIMINARY ITEMS

It is common for designated items to be paid for by a lump sum rather than for the full cost of staff, goods, plant stores and services to be reimbursable as prime cost. The JCT 87 system makes provision for this. Usually the items designated are ones for which the scope and amount required can be readily ascertained or predicted by the time the second part of the management contract is due to be executed (ie before the end of the pre-construction period).

Even where the cost of the designated items can be predicted, a lump sum represents some risk to the management contractor (he may miscalculate the lump sum, for instance, or the circumstances in which he supplies the designated items may significantly change). For this reason some management contracts (including the JCT Management Contract) allow adjustment of the lump sum for management contractor's preliminaries if certain events occur. The low-risk philosophy of pure management contracting is thus preserved whilst the employer receives some comfort from the likely lump sum price of the designated management contractor's preliminaries. However, if the lump sum for these items is too easily adjusted, there may be little advantage in having a lump sum at all as far as the employer is concerned. It is common for management contracts to specify a limited number of events which will cause adjustment to the lump sum.

3 MANAGEMENT CONTRACTOR'S FEES

As a result of the general structure of management contracts, the fee is often divided into two parts: a pre-construction fee referable to the pre-construction services, and a construction fee referable to the construction services. The latter is generally payable after Part 2 of the management contract has been entered into or the employer has told the management contractor to proceed with construction. However, in certain circumstances instalments of the two sections of the fee may appear in the same certificate.

The fees are most often calculated either as lump sum fees (adjustable in certain given circumstances) or as a percentage of the prime cost, subject to certain restrictions (see Section 4).

Whatever the method of calculation, it is advisable to make clear which items are included in the fee, even if this is only a reference to the fee being inclusive of all costs and expenses which are not otherwise reimbursable in the prime cost or payable as part of the lump sum for the management contractor's preliminaries. From the management contractor's viewpoint it is often preferable to list items included in the fee and specifically state that all other items not included as lump sum preliminaries are to be treated as part of the prime cost. This is consistent with the theory of management contracting as a low-risk method but, from the employer's point of view, it is another element of uncertainty and may become a bone of contention in a system intended to be less adversarial than traditional methods.

The following items may be considered in defining the fee:

- the management contractor's gross profit;
- the cost of management off-site including all the types of staff costs discussed in Section 1;
- off-site services provided at the management contractor's own offices and other overhead expenditure;
- the management contractor's capital employed in the project (including any interest);
- the cost of accounting including administration of VAT in connection with the works; and
- the cost of administering the works contracts.

4 ADJUSTMENT OF THE FEE AND TARGET COST CONTRACTS

A criticism often levelled at prime cost contracts is that, because the costs that the contractor incurs are reimbursable by the employer, there is little incentive for the contractor to take stringent measures to control the cost of the project. On the other hand, it is sometimes argued that fixed fees are a disincentive to good management, as the management contractor's profit remains static no matter how successfully he manages the project. It is also sometimes said that if an increased prime cost indicates that significant extra effort is required to manage the works, it is unfair that the management contractor's fee does not show a related increase.

Adjustable fee

Each of these arguments can lead to an agreement between the parties that the fee may be adjustable in certain circumstances. The JCT Management Contract suggests that the construction period fee should only be adjusted where there has been a 5% change in the prime cost from that in the contract cost plan total (although the percentage increase or decrease is open to the discretion of the parties). The adjustment formula means that if the prime cost increases by the specified percentage the fee also increases. Similarly, if the prime cost falls the fee may fall too. This is a 'step' adjustment rather than a sliding scale adjustment (ie there is no adjustment unless the agreed percentage of increase or decrease has been reached). The adjustment is made when costs overrun or change for any reason at all; the change does not have to be due to the architect's instructions.

An alternative to such schemes is to calculate the fee as a percentage of the prime cost. This has the same disadvantages (it appears to punish cost savings and encourage poor cost control) without the advantages of the percentage cost thresholds in the JCT suggested formula. In either case an employer may wish to limit the circumstances in which such adjustment may occur and will almost certainly wish to state that no increase is to be made where the cost increase is due to the management contractor's default. The employer may also hold that certain items which would otherwise form part of the prime cost (such as fluctuations payable to works contractors) may be excluded for the purposes of calculating the percentage fee.

Target cost mechanisms

It is believed in some quarters that the introduction of targets provides the incentive to the contractor that general prime cost linked with positively adjustable fee lacks.

Cost, time and quality are the principal elements of a project and targets may be applied to each of these. Target cost mechanisms have three key elements: the target cost (the estimate of the actual cost of the works), the target fee (the fee payable if the actual cost equals the target cost) and the method by which overruns or underruns of the actual cost against the target cost are apportioned between the management contractor and the employer.

The target cost should be the best estimate available of the prime cost. The amount of care taken in calculating it and the confidence of each party in its accuracy will be reflected in the percentage increase or decrease which is required before the fee adjusts. In addition, changes to the cost caused by certain events should not affect the fee. However, arranging this may involve providing a mechanism for adjustment of the target cost (for example, because of changes in the scope of the works).

After the percentage threshold of overrun or underrun is met, the target fee starts to decrease (for an overrun) or increase (for an underrun). The change may be worked out with a straight line sliding scale. Alternatively, it can be calculated on a weighted basis so that a small cost overrun causes a proportionately small decrease in the contractor's profits while an overrun that is 10 times more expensive attracts (say) a reduction in the fee that is 15 times more substantial. To ensure that incentive is not removed entirely or to prevent a wholly unrealistic target cost being put forward, it may be prudent to ensure that maximum and minimum levels of fee are agreed.

Specific adjustments to the fee are one way to provide incentives for cost control. Another is to have a fixed fee but also to provide a mechanism for sharing cost increases or decreases between the parties, with each bearing or receiving a fixed proportion of the overrun or underrun. Alternatively, a sliding scale of percentages may be applied to bands of differences between the target and actual cost. The sharing arrangement may sometimes be limited on the overrun side of target cost by the use of a guaranteed maximum sum. In this case, if actual costs rise to the level of the guaranteed maximum sum, the contract becomes a fixed price contract under which the employer does not reimburse any further costs.

It must be remembered that the introduction of a target mechanism into a low-risk management contract provides the management contractor with an incentive but also requires him to carry risk. It is important that the incentive is big enough to produce the desired effect in terms of effort and economy.

CHAPTER 10

TERMINATION AND INSOLVENCY

1 TERMINATION FOR NEUTRAL EVENTS

The termination clause may include the right to terminate the management contract because of neutral events such as force majeure or loss or damage caused to the project by a specified peril. In many cases, it will be preferable to insert a separate provision providing for termination by either party if any neutral events occur. This will enable the parties to give separate treatment to the cost consequences that arise in such circumstances. In the JCT Management Contract, for example, the management contractor is not entitled to recover any direct loss or damage if his employment is determined because of any neutral events.

2 TERMINATION BY THE EMPLOYER FOR CONVENIENCE

The management contractor is treated as part of the professional team rather than as a contractor. It is consistent with this approach that the employer has the right (as he has in the appointment of his consultants) to terminate 'for convenience' his relationship with the management contractor.

An employer may wish to terminate the management contractor's employment for a number of reasons. For example, he may find that having embarked on the design stage with the management contractor he cannot raise the funds to finance the project. He may be unable to obtain planning permission. Market conditions might have changed. A host of problems can arise to make it impossible to continue with the project or make the project no longer commercially viable.

Cost consequences

The cost of exercising this right of termination will depend on the stage at which the employer decides to act. It is possible to provide for varying cost consequences on termination but this is usually an expensive right to exercise.

The cost consequences can be treated in a number of ways. In the JCT Management Contract, for example, the cost consequences depend on whether termination takes place before or during the construction period.

If termination takes place during the construction period, the management contractor is paid as if he had determined his employment for an employer's default. He is entitled to his loss of profit. But if termination happens before the construction period begins, he is entitled to an appropriate proportion of the pre-construction period management fee, less any amount paid under an interim certificate.

An alternative approach is to provide that the management contractor is entitled to recover his loss of profit on a sliding scale, according to when termination takes place. In other words, the management contractor's right to recover his loss of profit can be directly linked to the prime cost incurred at the point of termination.

3 TERMINATION BY THE MANAGEMENT CONTRACTOR FOR EMPLOYER DEFAULT

If the employer is in default, the management contractor will normally have the right to determine his own employment by giving notice to the employer. There is usually a procedure which the management contractor must follow before he can determine his employment. It is particularly important that the management contractor complies fully with the procedural requirements. If he does not, his determination may be invalid and his conduct may therefore amount to a repudiation of the contract.

Grounds for termination

The JCT Management Contract, for example, lists four situations in which the management contractor can determine his employment. These are where the employer fails to pay a certificate; interferes with or obstructs the issue of any certificate; suspends the works due to his own acts or defaults; or is insolvent.

The employer fails to pay a certificate

Under the JCT Management Contract, the management contractor has the right to terminate where the employer does not pay 'the amount properly due' on any certificate. In these circumstances, the management contractor should be particularly careful before exercising his rights under this clause as the employer may be entitled to deduct sums or exercise a right of set-off.

The employer interferes with or obstructs the issue of any certificate

Any conduct of the employer calculated to influence the sums to be certified or the decision to be reached by the architect on a matter within the architect's sphere of discretionary duty would amount to interference or obstruction with the issue of a certificate. Such behaviour might constitute a breach of contract by the employer and this type of clause may therefore give the management contractor a right to terminate which he would not otherwise have at common law.

The employer suspends the works due to his own acts or defaults

As the management contractor's principal obligation is to co-operate with the employer's professional team, it is perhaps not appropriate to include such a provision, which effectively treats the management contractor as a contractor in a traditional form of contract rather than as a member of the employer's professional team. In the JCT Management Contract, for example, the events that give rise to a right to terminate under this clause (if they cause continuous suspension for a stipulated period) include instructions for changes, works contract variations, the expenditure of provisional sums and postponement instructions.

The employer is insolvent

The JCT Management Contract does not provide for automatic determination upon the employer's insolvency but states that the management contractor may determine his employment upon notice.

Cost consequences

When the management contractor's employment is determined, the employer will be obliged to pay the management contractor the prime costs the management contractor has incurred, including the costs of materials which have not yet been delivered to the site but for which he is legally bound to pay. The employer also has to pay the management contractor a proportion of his management fee, reasonable removal costs (including removal costs of the works contractors) and any direct loss or damage caused to the management contractor by the determination. This will include the direct loss or expense caused to works contractors which they will be entitled to claim from the management contractor under the terms of the works contract.

4 TERMINATION BY THE EMPLOYER FOR MANAGEMENT CONTRACTOR OR WORKS CONTRACTOR DEFAULT

At common law, an employer is entitled to regard a contract as brought to an end if the contractor's behaviour shows that he no longer has any intention of carrying out his contractual obligations. Such conduct by a contractor amounts to a repudiation of the contract. The employer must decide whether to accept the management contractor's repudiatory conduct as ending the contract and releasing him from any further performance or to hold the defaulting contractor to his contract and claim damages for the breach.

In practice, it is difficult for an employer to know with any certainty whether the contractor can be said to have repudiated his contract. The consequences of treating the contractor's conduct as amounting to repudiation if in fact it is not serious enough to be repudiatory will be significant. An employer will usually prefer to rely on his contractual rights to determine the management contract, rather than on his common law rights - not only because of the clearly-defined grounds which give rise to termination but also because of the benefits conferred upon the employer by such termination clauses.

The termination clause in a management contract will usually entitle the employer to terminate the management contractor's employment in the event of any default by the management contractor or a works contractor. In general, the aim of such a clause is to give the employer wider rights of termination than he would otherwise have at common law and to give him certain specific rights, in order to make it easier to complete the project following termination.

Grounds for termination

The circumstances that give rise to grounds for termination by the employer in the JCT Management Contract, for example, are as follows:

- where the management contractor suspends or fails to proceed regularly and diligently with the carrying out of his obligations;

- where the management contractor fails to comply with a notice relating to defective work or materials; and

- where the management contractor has assigned his contract without obtaining the employer's consent.

Regularly and diligently proceeding with the works

It will often be difficult to ascertain whether or not the management contractor is 'regularly and diligently' proceeding with the works. The phrase is easier to define in its application to a works contractor's duties, which involves physical work. The phrase has been considered in *Hounslow Borough Council v Twickenham Garden Developments Ltd* (1970) and in *Lintest Builders Ltd v Roberts* (1978), in the context of a contractor's duties. In these cases the court found the phrase elusive and expressed uncertainty as to the concept enshrined in the words. An employer would be ill-advised to determine the management contractor's employment on this ground, unless progress is so slow that there can be no prospect of the project being completed by the completion date or within a reasonable period.

The programme is a useful starting point in deciding whether the management contractor is proceeding with the works regularly and diligently. A failure on the management contractor's part to comply with the programme for the execution of the works, although not itself a breach of contract, may amount to prima facie evidence of failure to proceed regularly and diligently with the works. However, the management contractor may be able to show that he is entitled to an extension of time, or that the delay was caused by some act of the employer, or that some other programme that he is adhering to indicates that he is proceeding regularly and diligently.

Failure to comply with a notice

Unless the management contractor refuses or neglects to communicate the architect's instructions to the works contractor, it will in practice be difficult to determine the management contractor's employment for failing to comply with a notice relating to defective works or materials. If the works contractor fails to comply with such an instruction, the management contractor is unlikely to be in breach unless he fails to take steps to remind the works contractor of his obligations. Under the JCT Management Contract, the management contractor will only be in breach if the project is materially affected by the management contractor's default.

Notice given unreasonably or vexatiously

In the JCT Management Contract the termination clause is subject to the proviso that notice of termination may not be given by the employer 'unreasonably' or 'vexatiously'.

An identically worded proviso was considered by the Court of Appeal in *John Jarvis Ltd v Rockdale Housing Association* (1987). 'Unreasonably' was then held to be 'a general term which can include anything which can be objectively judged to be unreasonable'. A notice would not be considered as given unreasonably unless it was one which no reasonable employer in the circumstances of the particular employer would have given. 'Vexatiously' was said to connote 'an ulterior motive to oppress, harass, or annoy'. Whether a notice is unreasonable or vexatious will be a question of fact in each case.

Employer's rights on termination

Upon termination of the management contractor's employment for management contractor or works contractor default, the employer will acquire specific rights which will facilitate the completion of the project and which he would not otherwise have at common law. (It should be noted that most of these rights also arise on automatic termination due to insolvency - see Section 5.) The following rights will be particularly useful to him.

The right to use the management contractor's equipment and materials

The employer can only use the equipment which was owned by the management contractor at the date of termination. If the equipment is leased, hired or subject to retention of title clauses, then the employer will be unable to take over the plant or materials. If he tries to do so, he may be liable in the tort of conversion to pay damages to whichever third party has a claim on the equipment.

The JCT Management Contract also gives the employer the express right to employ and pay others to complete the obligations of the management contractor. This sort of express right is arguably unnecessary. Once the management contractor's employment has been determined, he has no interest in the further progress of the project other than the amount of any direct loss or damage caused to the employer by the determination.

The right to call for the assignment of the benefit of all contracts to the employer

This provision (which will not apply if determination arises automatically on insolvency - see Section 5) is designed to give the employer the benefit of works contracts and supply contracts until a new management contractor is appointed. However, the right to call for an assignment will be of limited value where there is an automatic termination provision. This difficulty arises in JCT Works Contract/2, under which the employment of the works contractor is automatically determined if the management contractor's employment is determined. Although the JCT Management Contract includes a mechanism for the employer to take an assignment of the works contract, there is nothing for the management contractor to assign other than his rights of action for past breaches of the works contract.

The automatic termination provisions in works contracts can also cause difficulties if the employer decides to reinstate the management contractor's employment. It then becomes necessary to discuss with the works contractor the terms upon which his employment is also to be reinstated.

The right to call for performance of an obligation can be assigned without consent if the contract is non-personal and has no prohibition against assignment. However, building contracts may or may not be characterised as personal contracts, depending on the particular circumstances. If the contract is non-personal, the benefit can be assigned as long as there is no prohibition against assignment. Where there is a requirement that assignment should not take place without consent, assignment without consent will be ineffective and will not pass either the right to call for performance or any contractual rights of action. (See *Linden Gardens Trust v Lenesta Sludge Disposals Ltd and Others* (1993).)

The right to make direct payments to works contractors or suppliers and to deduct such sums from amounts due to the management contractor

It should be noted that this provision will not apply if termination arises automatically upon insolvency (see Section 4).

The right to suspend any further payments to the management contractor until completion of the project

Under the JCT Management Contract it is not clear whether payments are suspended until practical completion or until the stage at which the final account is concluded. The latter stage seems more appropriate, as the architect will only then be in a position to certify the amount of expenses properly incurred by the employer and the direct loss or damage caused to him by the determination. However, the two decisions of His Honour Judge Newey QC in *HW Nevill (Sunblest) Ltd v William Press and Son Ltd* (1981) and in *Emson Eastern Ltd (In Receivership) v EME Developments Ltd* (1991) suggest that practical completion constitutes completion in the context of such a termination clause.

The right to claim and set off direct loss or damage

The employer may claim from the management contractor any direct loss and damage caused to the employer by the determination and set off that direct loss and damage against any sums that may become due to the management contractor by that determination.

The right to require the management contractor to remove all equipment from the site as and when required in writing by the architect, with appropriate provisions for the management contractor's failure to comply

In exercising this right, an employer should ensure that he does not dispose of hired or leased plant – something which could make him liable in the tort of conversion.

5 TERMINATION BY THE EMPLOYER FOR MANAGEMENT CONTRACTOR'S INSOLVENCY

The contract may provide that the management contractor's employment is automatically determined if he becomes insolvent (although it may be reinstated and continued if the employer and the contractor agree). Alternatively, the contract may provide for the management contractor's employment to be determined on notice.

It is important to remember that the management contractor's employment is determined, rather than the contract itself. Certain provisions in the contract will indicate the parties' rights and obligations if the management contractor's employment is ended because of his insolvency. The distinction was highlighted in the case of *Scobie & McIntosh Ltd v Clayton Bowmore Ltd* (1990). A sub-contractor was entitled to claim damages and was not restricted to the compensation provided for under the contract. The court held that the sub-contract had been repudiated and his employment under the sub-contract was not terminated.

Automatic determination

If the management contract contains an automatic termination provision, it is prudent for an employer who wishes to take advantage of the clause to inform the management contractor immediately that he is relying on the automatic termination. If the employer permits the works to continue, it may be argued that he has waived his rights under the clause and that the employment of the management contractor has been reinstated and continued.

The automatic termination provision can cause difficulties, particularly if the works contracts provide that the works contractors' employment is also terminated upon termination of the management contract. If the employer chooses to reinstate the management contractor's employment it will be necessary to discuss with each works contractor the terms upon which his employment is also to be reinstated. An employer may consider avoiding this problem by omitting the automatic determination provision and instead providing for termination upon notice.

The automatic termination provision may cause particular difficulties if a receiver is appointed, as the employer's interests may be better served by requiring a receiver to proceed with and complete the project, particularly if the project is nearing completion.

Employer's rights on termination

If the management contractor becomes insolvent and his employment has not been reinstated and continued, the employer acquires certain rights, already referred to in Section 4. However, an employer will not usually be able to call for the assignment of the benefit of the works contracts. Nor will he have the right to make direct payment to the works contractors. Furthermore, he may not deduct such payments from any sums due to the management contractor.

Direct payment clauses

The law of insolvency renders unenforceable any clause which provides that, if a company goes into liquidation, its assets are transferred to a third party rather than being made available to the liquidator. This is because of the pari passu rule that all unsecured creditors should receive equal treatment and that a company's assets should be distributed pro rata to the creditors' debt.

In *Re Wilkinson ex p Fowler* (1905), and in *Re Tout & Finch Ltd* (1954), direct payments by the employer to sub-contractors were held to be valid and exercisable by the employer against the contractor's liquidator who had continued the contract. However, the status of these cases has been uncertain since the case of *British Eagle International Airlines Ltd v Compagnie Nationale Air France* (1975). (See also the Singaporean case of *Joo Yee Construction Proprietary Ltd v Diethelm Industries Proprietary Ltd* (1991) and *Glow Heating Ltd v Eastern Health Board* (1992).)

British Eagle concerned the effect on direct payment clauses of Section 302 of the Companies Act 1948 (which now appears as Section 107 of the Insolvency Act 1986). The House of Lords held that any arrangement with creditors of a company will be ineffective if its result is that a creditor is paid other than in accordance with the order of payment prescribed by the law of insolvency.

Although the *British Eagle* case was not concerned with a direct payment clause, or indeed with building contracts in general, the JCT Management Contract has been drafted (like JCT 80) to provide expressly for the direct payment provision to cease on the management contractor's insolvency.

In general, it appears that direct payment clauses are valid against the management contractor's liquidator insofar as they purport only to operate prospectively and do not divert to sub-contractors money to which the management contractor is already legally entitled. However, it may be prudent for an employer to protect himself by seeking an indemnity from the works contractor, in case the employer has to pay the same amount - or any part of the direct payment - to the liquidator of the management contractor.

Certificates showing sums due to works contractors may also cover money which the management contractor is entitled (as between himself and the works contractor) to retain by way of retention. If the management contractor holds this money as trustee, it would seem that the employer could pay this direct to the works contractor if the management contractor is insolvent. The management contractor's only right to the money would be as the trustee for the works contractor. Accordingly, his liquidator or trustee in bankruptcy would have no substantial claim against the employer for it.

Administration orders

We have seen in Section 4 that on termination the employer will have the right to use the management contractor's equipment and materials to carry out and complete the project. It is not entirely clear what the effect of such a clause is if the contractor is the subject of an administration order under Section 11(3) of the Insolvency Act 1986, which prohibits any 'steps ... to enforce any security over the company's property ... or other proceedings ... execution or other legal process ... or distress against the company or its property'.

It is arguable that any attempt by an employer to make use of the management contractor's plant is a breach of Section 11(3). In *Exchange Travel v Triton Property* (1991), the court held that the phrase 'other security' was wide enough to cover a right of re-entry conferred on a landlord by the terms of the lease. Therefore, once an administration order was made, a landlord was precluded by Section 11(3) from exercising his right of re-entry without the consent of the administrator or the court. However, it appears that the position under a construction contract can be distinguished on the basis that the purpose of giving the employer a contractual right to use the contractor's plant and equipment is to enable him to complete the contract rather than to obtain security for its performance. In a lease, on the other hand, the right of re-entry is a security for the failure to pay rent.

Although the right to terminate is contractual in nature and is not a security interest or proprietary right requiring leave before it can be exercised, the termination clauses found in many standard form contracts give the employer the right of set-off and thus have a security function. As the spirit of the administration procedure is to suspend all rights that have a security function, it may be argued that extended termination clauses are unenforceable if the management contractor is in administration. However, these termination clauses may be valid, on the basis that the company in administration is bound by the terms of any existing contract. In practice, a court will also consider the terms of the construction contract when deciding whether or not an administration order is appropriate in all the circumstances.

CHAPTER 11

MANAGEMENT CONTRACTOR'S LIABILITY FOR WORKS CONTRACTORS

1 THE RELIEF CLAUSE

A distinguishing feature of management contracts is a contract term whose effect or intention is to relieve the management contractor of his normal absolute liability for breaches and defaults of the works contractors who are sub-contracted to him. It is this feature that creates the essentially low-risk nature of the contract for the management contractor. The low risk is reflected in the management contractor's fee and (according to the so-called philosophy of management contracting) his attitude to the project. (Interestingly the First Edition of the ICE's New Engineering Contract, published in 1993, departs from this principle by not including a relief provision for the management contractor in its management contract option.)

General examples

The general approach is somehow to subordinate the employer's right to recover compensation from the management contractor to the management contractor's entitlement and ability to recover compensation from his works contractors. This can be achieved in a variety of ways. Three examples, based on bespoke contract provisions encountered in practice, are given below.

Example A

The management contractor's liability to the employer is limited (in respect of matters sub-contracted by the management contractor to works contractors) to a liability to account to the employer for such sums as the management contractor may recover from the works contractor as a result of any breach or repudiation of the relevant works contract in accordance with that contract's terms. This liability to the employer exists only to the extent that the employer has suffered a loss because of such a breach or repudiation.

Here, the relief principle is a contractual limitation on the management contractor's liability. By virtue of Section 3 of the Unfair Contract Terms Act 1977, the relief principle may therefore be subject to the reasonableness requirement of the Act if used in the written standard terms of the business of the party relying on it (ie the management contractor). In practice, the relief principle will usually satisfy the reasonableness requirement. Section 11(1) of the Act defines the requirement as that:

> '... the term shall have been a fair and reasonable one to be included having regard to the circumstances which were, or ought reasonably to have been, known to or in the contemplation of the parties when the contract was made.'

These circumstances would probably include the intended nature and effect of the contract, in terms of the relatively low degree of risk intended to be placed on the management contractor in return for a relatively low percentage fee.

Example B

To the extent that the management contractor is liable to the employer in respect of any breach of the management contract or otherwise as a result of any breach by a works contractor of his works contract, then the management contractor will take reasonable steps to secure the works contractor's performance and recover damages in respect of the works contractor's breach, and the employer will not be entitled to enforce, under the terms of the management contract or otherwise, any right against the management contractor to damages in respect of the management contractor's liability, in excess of such sums (if any) as the management contractor shall have recovered and received from the works contractor or before recovery and receipt of such sums.

Here, the relief principle is expressed not as a limitation of the management contractor's liability but rather as a bar on the employer's entitlement to enforce rights which would otherwise arise under the management contract. This may make it a procedural matter (like a time bar under the Limitation Acts) rather than a means of defining the scope of the employer's contractual right and therefore limiting or extinguishing his cause of action.

Example C

Where the management contractor is liable to the employer for breach of the management contract by reason of any act or omission of the works contractor, the management contractor is to take all necessary steps to enforce the terms of the works contract and shall be reimbursed accordingly by the employer, and the employer shall not be entitled to recover from the management contractor any sums in excess of such sums (if any) as the management contractor shall have recovered and received from the works contractor, or before recovery and receipt of such sums.

This seems a clear restriction of the employer's remedy. It leaves the employer carrying the risk of non-recovery by the management contractor. As in example B, actual recovery and receipt are required, not merely an ability or an entitlement to recover. Consequently, actual payment by the works contractor is required, rather than merely the ability or obligation to pay.

A clause of this type was considered in *The Chester Grosvenor Hotel Company Ltd v Alfred McAlpine Management Ltd* (1992). His Honour Judge Stannard held that, in the circumstances of the case, the clause satisfied the requirement of reasonableness under the Unfair Contract Terms Act 1977. He also held that the claim did not afford the management contractor a defence for breach of such of its obligations as were unrelated to performance by the works contractors.

The JCT Management Contract Clause 3.21

In the JCT 87 system the relief principle is found in Clause 3.21 of the Management Contract. The following provisions of the JCT Management Contract (and only these) are expressly stated to be subject to Clause 3.21.

- The management contractor is to be fully liable to the employer for any breach of the terms of the contract, including any breach caused by a works contractor having breached his obligations under the relevant works contract (Clause 1.7).

- The management contractor is to secure the making good of all defects, shrinkages or other faults specified in the architect's schedule of defects, at no cost to the employer (Clause 2.5).

- The management contractor is to pay or allow the employer liquidated and ascertained damages for any period between the contractual completion date and the date on which work is actually completed (Clause 2.10).

- The management contractor is to comply with the architect's instructions in regard to the removal from the site of any work, materials or goods which are not in accordance with the contract, at no cost to the employer (Clause 3.11).

- The management contractor is to comply or secure compliance with the architect's instructions requiring the making good of any defect, shrinkage or other fault discovered at any time and due to materials, goods or workmanship not in accordance with the contract, at no cost to the employer (Clause 3.12).

These provisions cover the whole of the management contractor's normal basic obligations to the employer. These are equivalent to those of a traditional main contractor. In other words, the management contractor in principle is responsible for delays in completing the works and for defects in the works. He cannot delegate that responsibility to works contractors.

However, Clause 3.21 of the JCT Management Contract applies 'notwithstanding anything contained elsewhere in this contract' and 'in respect of any breach of, or non-compliance with, a works contract by a works contractor', including expressly a termination of the employment of a works contractor for default. Clause 3.21 therefore overrides all the rest of the contract, whether or not particular provisions are expressly subject to it.

Clause 3.21.2.3 is the core of the relief clause. It states that the employer shall be entitled to recover from the management contractor all amounts paid or credited to the management contractor under Clause 3.21.2.1, and where relevant the amount of liquidated and ascertained damages referred to in Clause 3.21.2.2, but only to the extent that such amounts have been recovered by the management contractor from the defaulting works contractor.

This is like example C above, in that it expresses a limitation on what the employer is 'entitled to recover' if a works contractor is in breach of his works contract. This was certainly the JCT's intention in drafting the clause. JCT Practice Note MC/1 says that the management contractor:

'... is obliged to seek from the works contractor in default all the costs that have resulted from that default including the amounts incurred by the employer; and the management contractor is bound to pay the employer what damages he has obtained from the defaulting works contractor but if there is any shortfall between these damages and what the employer has incurred *that shortfall is borne by the employer not the management contractor*' (JCT emphasis).

The effect of Clause 3.21

A closer examination of Clause 3.21 casts some doubt on whether (and how) the intended effect is achieved.

To begin with, the preamble of Clause 3.21 states simply that its provisions shall apply 'in respect of any breach of or non-compliance with a Works Contract by a Works Contractor'. (This is deemed to include termination of the works contractor's employment for default.) The clause does not expressly apply to a breach of contract by the *management contractor* caused or constituted by the works contractor's breach.

It is true that Clause 3.21 is said to apply 'notwithstanding anything contained elsewhere in this Contract'. Furthermore, Clause 1.7 (which is expressly subject to Clause 3.21) states explicitly the principle that the management contractor's liability to the employer for breach of his contract includes any breach occasioned by a works contractor's breach of his works contract. However, the same principle would apply even without this affirmation.

This general principle can be expressly excluded. But its exclusion by Clause 3.21 seems, at best, implied. As an exclusion, it will in any case be construed contra proferentem if (as sometimes happens) Clause 3.21 is used as the basis for a bespoke form of management contract put forward by the management contractor. Without the implied exclusion, Clause 3.21 could be taken as merely elaborating certain mandatory procedural steps to be followed by the employer and the management contractor if a works contractor is in breach of his works contract. It could be read as dealing principally with the means by which and the degree to which the management contractor is to pursue his remedies against the works contractor, as well as the extent to which he is to be reimbursed for doing so and the accounts for and timing of payment of liquidated damages if the works contractor's breach consists of a delay.

There are also points where it is difficult to reconcile the substantive provisions of Clause 3.21. As noted above, Clause 3.21.2.3 is the core of Clause 3.21. It limits what the employer would otherwise be entitled to recover from the management contractor with the words 'entitled to recover ... but only to the extent that such amounts had been recovered by the Management Contractor from the Works Contractor who is in breach ...'. It refers to amounts 'paid or credited to' the management contractors under Clause 3.21.2.1.

However, Clause 3.21.2.1 refers to amounts 'incurred by' the management contractor, including specifically any amount for which the management contractor is liable under Clause 1.7 (through his expressed liability for works contractors' breaches). It is hard to see how these can be amounts to which the limitation on the employer's entitlement to recovery under Clause 3.21.2.3 applies. This means that the only amounts to which that limitation can apply are the 'liquidated and ascertained damages referred to in Clause 3.21.2.2' (ie normal liquidated damages due under Clauses 2.10 and 2.11 for delay in completion).

It seems that no other provision in Clause 3.21 or elsewhere in the JCT Management Contract expressly restricts the employer's right to recover general damages for breaches by the management contractor, even where they are brought about by a works contractor's breach. Clause 3.21.3 requires the employer to reimburse the management contractor for certain shortfalls, but only those caused by the management contractor having to meet claims by one works contractor arising from breaches by another works contractor.

It seems possible that the management contractor may thus remain liable to the employer for general damages resulting from breaches of the management contractor's general obligations under the JCT Management Contract (other than those covered by liquidated damages for delay). However, the management contractor can still recover from the employer the costs he incurs in recovering damages from the defaulting works contractor. These cover the management contractor's own loss and damage as well as the employer's.

2 EFFECT OF RELIEF CLAUSE ON EMPLOYER'S REMEDIES

The aim of putting any relief clause (including the JCT Management Contract Clause 3.21) in a management contract is to ensure that the employer can recover the amount of his losses resulting from a works contractor's breach *only* if the management contractor can recover that amount from a works contractor under a works contract. If the employer is to recover all his losses, the amount of the management contractor's liability to the employer therefore needs to be both recoverable and recovered by the management contractor from the works contractor. Recovery may be achieved by way of proved foreseeable damages for breach of contract or through an obligation on the works contractors to indemnify the management contractor against this liability.

Indemnities from works contractors are dealt with in Sections 3 and 4. However, we must first consider some problems associated with the management contractor's need to prove foreseeable damage.

Potential difficulties

There are at least three ways in which problems can arise. All of them stem from the possibility that the sum for damage sustained by the employer as a result of the management contractor's breach may, in whole or part, be irrecoverable by the management contractor as damages from the works contractor. These situations are where there is no loss; discrepancy of loss; or dispersion of loss between works contractors.

No loss

This problem can theoretically arise whenever one party's recovery depends on another's title to sue and that other has itself no need of recovery.

Under a management contract with an effective relief provision, the management contractor is not liable for a loss to the employer caused by a works contractor's breach unless he can recover the loss himself from a works contractor. He can only recover from the works contractor a loss he has himself sustained. The only way he can sustain a legally-recoverable loss equivalent to that suffered by the employer is by being obliged to pay that amount to the employer. However, he is not obliged to do so unless and until he recovers it from the works contractor. But perhaps he cannot recover it from the works contractor because he has not yet had to pay it to the employer. And so on.

Possible ways of breaking this circle are considered in Section 3. The root of the problem is the essential difference between the management contract and the works contract, which are not in all respects 'back to back'. That difference is created by the very introduction of the relief provision into the management contract, as well as by the fact that the management contract will cover a wider range of works and performance than any one works contract.

The idea of a chain of contracts and sub-contracts where the measure of damages for breach at one level passes all the way along the chain as the measure of damages for breach of every contract in the chain is not unique to management contracting or even to construction contracts generally. However, in order for the same measure of damages to reach from one end of the chain to the other, there should be no material variation between all the contracts forming the chain. If there is a material variation, the requirement of foreseeability of damage is not satisfied (*Biggin & Co Ltd v Permanite Ltd* (1951), following *Dexters Ltd v Hill Crest Oil Co (Bradford) Ltd* (1926)).

Discrepancy of loss

The recovery of damages in contract depends on the principles of remoteness of damage established in *Hadley v Baxendale* (1854), as restated and clarified in *Victoria Laundry (Windsor) v Newman Industries* (1949). As stated by Asquith LJ in *Victoria Laundry*, the test is one of reasonable foreseeability, and what is reasonably foreseeable depends on actual or imputed knowledge of circumstances.

The management contractor's actual knowledge of the background and circumstances of the project will usually be greater than that of any individual works contractor. Depending on the closeness of any particular works contractor's involvement, particularly at the early stages of a project, his imputed knowledge of the background and circumstances may more or less approximate to that of the management contractor. However, it seems inevitable that there will be at least some difference between their respective states of knowledge, whether imputed or actual. In many cases this difference will be material.

In such instances, the degree of foreseeability, and thus the application of the test of remoteness of damage, will be different as between management contractor and employer and between management contractor and works contractor. Leaving aside the 'no loss' conundrum discussed above, the management contractor therefore may be unable to claim the same amount of damages from the works contractor as the employer could expect to claim from the management contractor in the absence of the relief provision.

Dispersion of loss among works contractors

The relief provision in a management contract is normally expressed by reference to a breach by a single works contractor of his works contract. For example, the JCT Management Contract Clause 3.21 applies 'in respect of any breach of or non-compliance with a Works Contract by a Works Contractor'; the clause then refers to 'the Works Contractor who is in breach'.

However, in practice, a breach of the obligations under the management contract will frequently be caused by a combination of breaches of works contracts or even by the interaction of a number of breaches. It may be difficult to allocate the full causation of a problem of quality or timing between several breaches. It may be equally difficult to quantify the precise damage resulting from one breach when it is one of several contributory breaches. It is quite possible that in such cases the total of the employer's loss and damage will be more than the sum of the several amounts recoverable by the management contractor from the various contributing works contractors.

The same situation exists under a construction management system where the employer engages the trade contractors directly and takes the risk of any gaps in provable liability between them. It is equally the case in matters of design responsibility (whether in connection with a traditional main contract or a management contract) where the employer directly engages several different consultant members of the design team. However, the fact that this is so highlights one of the essential differences between a management contract and a traditional main contract: a management contract does not provide a single point of liability to the employer for failure in contractual performance, as the traditional contract does.

3 DEVICES TO MAKE THE RELIEF CLAUSE WORK

Management contract systems commonly adopt two devices to try to overcome the difficulties mentioned above. The root of the problem lies in the scope of the works contractor's liability and in the management contractor's potential difficulty in proving that liability. So these two devices are included in the form of works contract.

Prohibition on arguing 'no loss'

The common solution to the 'no loss' conundrum is for the works contract to try simply to prevent the works contractor from raising the issue at all. This is stated in Clause 1.6.2 of JCT Works Contract/2 as follows:

> 'The Works Contractor, having notice of the terms of the Management Contract ... undertakes not to contend, whether in proceedings or otherwise, that the Management Contractor has suffered or incurred no damage, loss or expense or that his liability to the Management Contractor should be in any way reduced or extinguished by reason of clauses 3.21 and 3.22 of the Management Contract Conditions.'

Commentators have expressed doubt about the efficacy of such a provision. Some have supported it on the grounds that, as between the works contractor and the management contractor, the provisions of the management contract are res inter alios acta. At least the issue must arise of whether, as a matter of pleading, the works contractor can be put to making the 'no loss' contention in the first place. In any proceedings for recovery of the employer's losses, the management contractor will have to plead and prove these as losses he has suffered. He may be unable to do this if he has not in fact suffered the loss because he has not yet had to pay the employer. Even if he does plead it as a loss, the works contractor may simply not admit, rather than deny it, possibly not infringing a provision such as JCT Works Contract/2 Clause 1.6.2. However, if the clause is ever put to the test, a 'purposive' judicial interpretation might hold otherwise.

There is a further possibility. The 'no loss' question was addressed, in the rather different context of assignment, in the combined cases of *Linden Garden Trust v Lenesta Sludge Disposals Ltd* and *St Martin's Property Corporation Ltd v Sir Robert McAlpine & Sons Ltd* (1993). The House of Lords held that, even if an assignment of rights under a building contract is itself ineffective because the contract contains an effective prohibition on assignment, the assignor may still be entitled to damages from the contractor for losses the assignee incurs, on the basis of an old rule from mercantile law. The rule is formulated so that in a commercial contract, if it can be said to be in the contemplation of the parties that property in goods or property may be passed from the original buyer to another after the contract has been entered into but before the breach has occurred, then the original buyer, if both parties so intend, is to be treated as having contracted for the benefit of anyone who has or may acquire an interest in the goods or property before they are damaged (or lost). The original buyer may recover the loss sustained by those for whose benefit the contract was made. This remedy is only available where no other remedy is available to the person sustaining the loss. The assignor would be accountable later to the assignee.

It may be argued that this applies by analogy to the management contractor's relationship with the employer and amounts paid by the employer in remedying a works contractor's breach. However, if the employer has a direct right of action against a works contractor (eg by means of a collateral warranty) then this route will not be open.

Works contractor's liability equals management contractor's liability

The second device used to address the 'no loss' question also aims at the problem of potential discrepancy of loss. An express statement equating the works contractor's liability with that of the management contractor is included in the contract. It is coupled with an indemnity given by the works contractor against the management contractor's liability arising from the works contractor's default. Thus, in JCT Works Contract/2 Clause 1.6.1:

'The Works Contractor shall be fully liable to the Management Contractor for any breach of the terms of the Works Contract. Such liability shall include, but shall not be limited to, any liability which the Management Contractor may incur to the Employer under or for breach of the Management Contract by reason of the negligence, act, omission or default of the Works Contractor.'

Clause 1.8 says:

'The Works Contractor shall indemnify and save harmless the Management Contractor against any negligence or act or omission or default of the Works Contractor his agents or sub-contractors which involves the Management Contractor in any liability to the Employer under the provisions of the Management Contract.'

This indemnity is essentially the same as that used in forms of traditional sub-contract under a traditional main contract such as JCT NSC/4 or the Building Employers' Confederation Form DOM/1.

The statement of the works contractor's liability in Clause 1.6.1 of JCT Works Contract/2 is paralleled in Clause 1.7 of the Management Contract by an equivalent statement of the management contractor's liability.

> 'Subject to clause 3.21 the Management Contractor shall be fully liable to the Employer for any breach of the terms of this Contract including any breach occasioned by the breach by any Works Contractor of his obligation under the relevant Works Contract.'

Since the works contractor is on notice of the terms of Clause 1.7 of the Management Contract, this may be thought to fall within the words 'any liability which the Management Contractor *may incur* to the Employer' for the purposes of Clause 1.6.1 of JCT Works Contract/2. Once the management contractor can show the amount of the employer's loss, demonstrate that he has a potential liability to the employer for that loss and prove that the breach is occasioned by a works contractor's breach of the works contract, only an unduly strict interpretation would hold that the management contractor cannot recover damages from the works contractor because he has not yet actually incurred his liability by being obliged to pay the employer. The liability is still one which the management contractor 'may incur' to the employer. To hold otherwise would be to read 'may incur' in (for instance) JCT Works Contract/2 Clause 1.6.1 as 'may have incurred'. However, the position may be different when it comes to relying on the works contractor's *indemnity* as opposed to a claim for damages by the management contractor.

Discrepancy of loss

The management contractor's potential damages claim under a provision like JCT Works Contract/2 Clause 1.6.1 may address the 'no loss' difficulty referred to above. However, it will not deal with any discrepancy of loss. The extent of the management contractor's liability to the employer must be reasonably foreseeable by the works contractor, even if it is still only a liability which the management contractor 'may incur'. It will otherwise be too remote for the management contractor to be able to recover it as damages.

Such problems of remoteness of damage can only be dealt with by the works contractor's indemnity. Possible difficulties with this indemnity are considered in Section 4.

Dispersion of loss

Management contracts do not normally deal with the dispersion of the employer's loss between different works contractors, the third kind of problem affecting the employer's remedies discussed in Section 2. However, as previously noted, this does not leave the employer in a worse position than if he himself directly engages a number of different works contractors.

4 INDEMNITY FROM WORKS CONTRACTORS

If the works contractor agrees to indemnify the management contractor against his liability to the employer, the management contractor (and thus in turn the employer) will not face the difficulty of proving foreseeable damage.

An indemnity covers all actual loss caused by the act or omission against which the indemnity has been given. JCT Works Contract/2 Clause 1.8 defines this as any act 'which involves the Management Contractor in any liability to the Employer under the provisions of the Management Contract'. (Clause 5.2 of the JCT form of nominated sub-contract NSC/4 contains a similar definition.)

However, difficulties are still associated with indemnities against the liability of another. As in other areas, the common law adopts a restrictive technical view while equity may apply a more relaxed treatment.

Common law position

In principle, an obligation to indemnify another against the liability of a third party arises only after liability has been incurred and the indemnified party's resulting actual loss has been ascertained through its having made a payment to the third party. In *Biggin & Co Ltd v Permanite Ltd* (1951), although subsequently reversed in the Court of Appeal on other grounds, Devlin J stated that:

> 'The general rule is that a defendant who is required to indemnify a plaintiff against its liability to a third party is entitled to have the existence and precise extent of that liability proved against him in proceedings to which he is a party.'

In other words, at common law, the right to be indemnified can arise only when the event against which a party is indemnified has actually occurred. Where the indemnity is in respect of a liability to a third party, the event being indemnified against is the act of payment pursuant to that liability, not the act or omission giving rise to the liability.

This position was endorsed by Neill J in *Telfair Shipping Corp v Intersea Carriers* (1985), when he reviewed several authorities on the issue of when the cause of action on an indemnity arises for limitation purposes. (See *County & District Properties Ltd v C Jenner & Son Ltd* (1976); *R & H Green and Silley Weir Ltd v British Railways Board* (1985); *Gromal (UK) Ltd v WT Shipping Ltd* (1984); *Grand Bahama Petroleum Co Ltd v Manunited Companiera Naviera SA* (1985).)

Of these cases, *County & District Properties* concerned the indemnity in Clause 3(b) of the NFBTE 'green form' contract (a forerunner of JCT Works Contract/2 Clause 1.8). Swanwick J specifically held that clause to amount to an indemnity not against the liability arising but against the sustaining of ascertained loss resulting from the liability. *Scott Lithgow Ltd v Secretary of State for Defence* (1989) was a shipbuilding case in which it was held that the MoD's obligation to indemnify for damage became enforceable when the damage occurred, not when the shipbuilder's claim was submitted. However, this may perhaps be distinguished on the ground that the matters which were alleged to be conditions precedent to the indemnity claim were held to be mainly procedural or administrative in character.

It follows that at common law the effectiveness of the works contractor's indemnity clause (such as that in JCT Works Contract/2 Clause 1.8) may be doubtful. It may still be possible to argue that the management contractor's loss recoverable from the works contractor has not been ascertained (and thus has not triggered the obligation to indemnify) until the management contractor has actually paid out to the employer. But under the relief clause, the management contractor has no obligation to pay the employer until he has recovered the amount from the works contractor.

Treatment in equity

Equity has taken a less rigid view of indemnities. The issue was considered by the House of Lords in some depth in 1990 in the combined cases of *The Padre Island* and *The Fanto*, which concerned third party rights in marine insurance (*Firma C-Trade SA v Newcastle Protection and Indemnity Association* and *Socony Mobile Oil Inc v West of England Ship Owners Mutual Insurance Association (London) Ltd* (1991)).

It was argued in *The Padre Island* that although at common law an indemnity would only protect the indemnified person against actual loss incurred through payment, equity would go further and in appropriate circumstances require the indemnifier either to pay the creditor direct or to pay the indemnified person before he had paid the creditor. The case was eventually decided on the basis of an express contractual term requiring prior payment as a condition of indemnification, so remarks concerning the equitable relief contended for were strictly obiter. They are nevertheless of assistance. Lord Brandon stated:

'At law the party to be indemnified had to discharge the liability himself first and then sue the indemnifier for damages for breach of contract. In equity an ordinary contract of indemnity could be directed to be specifically performed by ordering that the indemnifier should pay the amount concerned direct to the third party to whom the liability was owed or in some cases to the party to be indemnified ... since the passing of the Supreme Court of Judicature Acts 1873 and 1875, the equitable remedy has prevailed over the remedy at law.'

Lord Goff confirmed this:

'Equity does not mend men's bargains; but it may grant specific performance of a contract, consistently with its terms, where the remedies at law are inadequate. This is what has happened in the case of contracts of indemnity. As a general rule, "equity requires that the party to be indemnified shall never be called upon to pay" (see *In Re Richardson* (1911)) and it is to give effect to that underlying purpose of the contract that equity intervenes, the common law remedies being incapable of achieving that result.'

These remarks raise the possibility of a remedy of specific performance for the management contractor to enforce the works contractor's indemnity, where the management contractor can prove the amount of the employer's loss for which he is liable under the management contract, but has not yet paid it over to the employer.

However, there are still some reasons for treating the prospect of such an equitable solution to the 'no loss' conundrum with caution. The cases on the common law position referred to above seem not to have been cited to the House of Lords in *The Padre Island*. In particular, in the *Telfair Shipping* case, Neill J considered the case of *In Re Richardson*, referred to by Lord Goff in *The Padre Island*. Neill J drew the opposite conclusion by reference to the judgment in that case of Fletcher Moulton LJ, which Lord Goff did not consider.

'The rule in Chancery was somewhat different and yet ... it emphasised the fundamental principle that you must have paid before you have a right to indemnity, because the remedy which equity gave was a declaration of a right. You could file a bill against the principal debtor to make him pay the debt so that you would not be called upon to pay it, and then you obtained a declaration that you were entitled to an indemnity. You could in certain cases have a fund set aside in order that you might be indemnified, to avoid the necessity of your having to pay and then sue for the money you had paid, which would perhaps not repair your loss and credit even if it discharged the debt. But I do not think that equity ever compelled a surety to pay money to the person to whom he was surety before the latter had actually paid. He might be ordered to set a fund aside, but I do not think that he could be ordered to pay.'

Given that their Lordships' remarks in *The Padre Island* were obiter, there must therefore still be some doubt about how far equity would go in enforcing payment under the works contractor's indemnity where the management contractor, relying on the relief provision, has not yet paid the employer.

Furthermore, even if equity provides a remedy where common law does not, the remedy will only be available if all those involved comply with equitable principles. The employer's remedy would therefore still depend, for instance, on the management contractor 'coming to equity with clean hands'.

5 EFFECT OF RELIEF CLAUSE AFTER FINAL CERTIFICATE

Our discussion of management contract relief provisions has assumed that their effect (whatever it may be) is at least applicable uniformly to any situation where the management contractor is liable to the employer for breach of the management contract and where that breach is connected with the liability of a works contractor to the management contractor for breach of a works contract. This situation may arise (that is to say, the breach may become apparent) either during the course of construction; or after practical completion but before the final certificate; or at any time after the issue of the final certificate (and before expiry of the limitation period).

The management contracting system apparently intends that the relief provision should be capable of operation at any of these stages. The philosophy behind the system is that there should be a low-risk contract for the management contractor, because only this will promote the advantages that the system is designed to bring about. The contract must remain one of low risk for the management contractor, whenever the question of his liability under it arises.

However, it may be argued that the relief provision may cease to have effect once all the practical obligations under the contract have been accomplished and all that remains is the potential monetary obligation for breach - in other words, upon issue of the final certificate. This argument depends on the true construction of the relief clause in question.

To take the abstract examples of relief clause quoted in Section 1, relief clauses formed along any of these lines would (probably) be effective, whether the management contractor's liability arose before or after the issuing of the final certificate. (Naturally, however, concrete expressions of these abstract clauses may include further express limiting provisions.)

Example A was expressed in terms of an outright limitation on the management contractor's liability to the employer. As with any other express contractual limitation of liability, such as a limitation to a fixed monetary amount or to a fixed type of loss or damage, this would apply whenever the potential liability is alleged or called in issue.

Example B was expressed as a bar on the employer enforcing a right to damages he might otherwise have had. In principle, this too could apply whenever the employer tries to enforce his right to damages.

Example C was expressed as a negation of the employer's right to recover more from the management contractor than the management contractor recovered from the defaulting works contractor. In principle, again, and subject to express contractual words to the contrary, this would apply at whatever time the employer attempts recovery.

JCT Management Contract – Clause 3.21

The relief clause in Clause 3.21 of the JCT Management Contract is more difficult to fit into this straightforward mould. Commentators have suggested that the detail of the activities referred to in Clause 3.21 (and in Clause 3.22) is aimed exclusively at matters that need to be dealt with before the final certificate is issued. They argue that the relieving or limiting provisions of Clause 3.21 are thus not intended to have effect after the final certificate. For instance, Clause 3.21.1 requires the management contractor to consult with the architect or contract administrator. But there will be no such person in office once the project is finished. Similarly, under Clause 3.21.1.2, the management contractor has to secure satisfactory completion of the project. But by definition, the project is completed in a practical sense once the final certificate is issued.

We believe this view to be at odds with the intention of Clause 3.21 and the effect of the JCT Management Contract as a whole, given the development of the standard form in the context of the growth of management contracting and the JCT's references to it in Practice Note MC/1. We also suggest that this view is not in fact borne out by the substance of Clause 3.21.

In the first place, the preamble to the clause states that it shall apply in respect of any breach of a works contract by a works contractor. A breach will normally only occur at the time of performance or completion of the works under a works contract. But it may not become apparent until considerably later. There is nothing to suggest that the preamble refers only to a works contract breach which happens to be discovered before the issue of the final certificate.

Secondly, Clause 3.21.1.1 requires the management contractor to take all necessary steps to operate the terms of the works contract for dealing with such breaches, including if necessary enforcement through arbitration or litigation. The process of arbitration or litigation will probably extend beyond the date on which the final certificate is issued – indeed, it may not even have begun by then (and there is nothing in the clause to suggest that it *should* have begun by then).

The reference in Clause 3.21.1.2 to securing 'the satisfactory completion of the project' is subject to the general qualification in Clause 3.21.1 that all 'necessary steps' be taken. In other words, it is not a mandatory provision but is only to be operated if applicable. Once the final certificate has been issued it will simply be inapplicable. Furthermore, Clause 3.21.1.3 requires the management contractor to meet any claims properly made under JCT Works Contract/2 by works contractors other than the works contractor in breach. There is nothing in JCT Works Contract/2 to suggest that those works contractors will be barred from making any such claims against the management contractor after the issue of the final certificate under the Management Contract.

Finally, Clauses 3.21.2 and 3.21.3 require the employer to meet the costs incurred by the management contractor in fulfilling his obligations under Clause 3.21.1 and to pay any shortfall in the amount recovered by the management contractor from a defaulting works contractor in respect of resultant claims by innocent works contractors. There is nothing to suggest that the employer's obligation to make such payments or reimbursement would cease on issue of the final certificate.

In fact, if there is any doubt about the effectiveness of the relief provision in Clause 3.21 from the management contractor's point of view, it probably arises because of the rather complicated drafting and cross-referencing within Clause 3.21 as mentioned in Section 1. A literal rather than purposive judicial interpretation might hold that the clause did not entirely achieve the JCT's stated intention. However, even the most literal interpretation seems unlikely to establish a cut-off point for whatever effect the clause does have, whether at the time of the final certificate or at any time other than the expiry of the relevant limitation period.

6 POSITION BETWEEN EMPLOYER AND WORKS CONTRACTORS

Employer/works contractor agreements

As far as the employer is concerned, works contractors under a management contract occupy the same position as sub-contractors under a traditional main contract. Their immediate principal contractual relationship is with the management contractor rather than the employer. The employer has no rights against a works contractor other than those available under the general law or those for which he stipulates in a specific contract with the works contractor. Following *Murphy v Brentwood DC* (1991), the employer's remedies in tort against a works contractor are severely limited. In any case, these remedies will only be available if the works contractor is negligent and not if he simply fails to comply with the works contract.

We have already mentioned that the employer's remedies against the management contractor for works contractors' breaches of works contracts may also be limited in effect because of the relief provision in the management contract. It is thus common practice for the employer to require direct agreements with the works contractors in order to establish a direct contractual remedy. These agreements are also common in circumstances where a traditional main contractor may not be fully liable to an employer for the performance of sub-contractors, such as situations involving nominated sub-contractors. In the JCT 87 scheme, the direct employer/works contractor agreement is Works Contract/3.

Given the difficulties discussed earlier, a direct agreement may be the only real source of recourse for an employer suffering loss through the default of a works contractor. For this reason, a direct agreement will be equally relevant to all works contractors, not only those (as suggested by JCT Practice Note MC/2) with some design responsibility. There may be grounds for making exceptions for works contract packages whose values are minimal in terms of the value of the project as a whole, but the potential knock-on effect of even a minimal package needs to be considered in relation to other packages. Direct agreements may need to be sought with all works contractors except any whose works are clearly severable from the rest of the project in terms both of timing and of compliance with specification.

If an employer/works contractor agreement is to make good the possible deficiency of the employer's remedies via the management contractor against the works contractor, it will have to oblige the works contractor to the employer in all aspects of his performance. The agreement is thus likely to cover the performance in general of the works contractor's obligations under his principal agreement with his direct employer (ie the management contractor). This will apply to materials, workmanship and any design carried out by the works contractor. The problems caused by an omission in the scope of a contract between an employer and a sub-contractor were exemplified in *Greater Nottingham Co-operative Society v Cementation Piling and Foundations Ltd* (1988). Damage was caused by the negligent workmanship of a sub-contractor's operative, but the form of agreement between the employer and the sub-contractor did not cover workmanship. It is worth noting that the JCT Works Contract/3 form of agreement between employer and works contractor retains this form.

To cover the deficiency in remedies available via the management contractor, an effective employer/works contractor agreement should impose an absolute performance obligation rather than merely an obligation to use reasonable care. An exception is likely to be made in the case of *design* undertaken by the works contractor, where the principal obligation is usually limited expressly to reasonable care. However, a works contractor undertaking what is in effect a direct design and build obligation to an employer may find his obligation classified as absolute (as in *Independent Broadcasting Authority v EMI Electronics Ltd and BICC Construction Ltd* (1980)) unless it is limited expressly to the standard of professional responsibility (as in Clause 2.5.1 of the JCT 81 design and build form).

As well as expressing some kind of direct right for the employer in relation to substantial performance by the works contractor, the agreement between employer and works contractor will normally express certain additional rights and obligations. In particular, it may create an express obligation for the works contractor to provide any design information in time to enable the architect to issue necessary instructions in good time to the management contractor. For example, JCT Works Contract/3 contains such an obligation for the works contractor but JCT Works Contract/2 does not impose a similar obligation between the works contractor and the management contractor.

The agreement may also contain an obligation on the employer to facilitate final payment to the works contractor according to a timescale related to the works contractor's own works rather than to the project as a whole. Any such obligation would normally be contingent on the employer being satisfied that the management contractor has been adequately indemnified by the works contractor against defects appearing in the works contractor's works after such an advanced final payment.

Privity of contract

In November 1991, the Law Commission published a consultation paper recommending that aspects of the law on privity of contract be reformed (Law Commission Consultation Paper number 121 - *Privity of contract: contracts for the benefit of third parties*). Its principal recommendation (subject to the consultation exercise) is that the law should be reformed, through a detailed legislative scheme, to allow third parties to enforce contractual provisions made in their favour. It provisionally recommends that a third party should be able to enforce a contract in which the parties intend that he should receive the benefit of the promised performance and also intend to create a legal obligation which he can enforce. It also recommends that the required intention be capable of being deduced from the surrounding circumstances rather than needing to be expressed (paragraphs 5.8 to 5.15 of the consultation paper).

If this recommendation were to become law it could have a considerable effect on the peculiar tripartite contractual structure created by a management contract system between employer, management contractor and works contractor. It should not be very difficult to deduce an intention on the part of the management contractor and works contractor that the employer should be entitled to rely on the benefit of the performance promised by the works contractor to the management contractor. No doubt express provisions could be incorporated, at the behest of employers, to avoid any uncertainty about the intentions of the parties.

Such a change in the law could go some way to alleviating the difficulties caused by the relief provisions in management contracts. However, it would not necessarily obviate the need for direct employer/works contractor agreements to give the works contractor the benefit of any direct obligation of the employer and to address any aspects of the works contractor's performance not covered by the works contract itself (as may be the case, for example, with works contractors' designs).

The Law Commission has received a substantial response to its consultation paper and has indicated that it may publish a report in 1994.

CHAPTER 12

MANAGEMENT CONTRACTOR'S RELATIONSHIP WITH WORKS CONTRACTORS

1 THE SELECTION OF WORKS CONTRACTORS AND THE FORM OF WORKS CONTRACTS

Selection of works contractors

As the management contractor has the skill and experience to assess the suitability of the works contractors, it is normally one of his basic obligations to identify suitable works contractors. It is also appropriate that he, rather than the architect, should play a leading role in the process of selection, as his responsibilities for the works contractors' defaults (although subject to the relief clause) are broader than the responsibilities of a main contractor for the defaults of a nominated sub-contractor in a traditional form of contract.

The employer will usually wish to retain some control over the selection process by providing that the selection of the works contractors is made by agreement between the architect and the management contractor. The contract may also provide that the architect's agreement must be confirmed by an architect's instruction issued under the management contract.

Agreed form of works contract

As the management contract and the works contracts are very closely interrelated, and as the employer's remedies depend upon the management contractor's remedies under the works contracts, it is important that amendments are not made to the agreed form of works contracts without the employer's prior approval. Amendments may have significant consequences for the management contract which may not be appreciated at the time the amendment is made. For this reason, an obligation is often imposed upon the management contractor to procure the works contracts in an agreed form.

Under the JCT Management Contract, for example, the management contractor cannot sign a works contract containing any amendments to the standard form unless the employer agrees to the amendments (Clause 8.2). The sanction against amending the works contract without consent is contained in the Second Schedule to the Management Contract, which has a definition of prime cost payable to the management contractor. Part 2 of the Second Schedule provides that the management contractor will not be reimbursed the amounts due and payable under the respective works contracts unless they are in the agreed form and comply with the provisions of Section 8.

The management contractor's failure to procure a works contract in the agreed form will have far-reaching effects on his rights and on the obligations he owes to the employer. In particular, the management contractor may lose the benefit of the relief provision if the works contracts are not in the agreed form. In the JCT Management Contract, for example, the relief provision contained in Clause 3.21 applies to any breach of, or non-compliance with, a works contract (which is defined as a contract which complies with Clause 8.2 - in other words, is in an agreed form). Under the JCT 87 scheme, failure to procure a works contract in an agreed form will therefore involve the management contractor in assuming all the risks which would otherwise be borne by the employer as a result of the relief provision.

Letters of intent

In practice, the works are often begun on the strength of letters of intent before either the management contractor or the works contractors have actually signed a contract. An employer and management contractor will often wish to proceed with the works expeditiously and it may be that the works contracts (and even the management contract) are not signed until the works are well underway.

If this happens, the management contractor may not have the benefit of any relief provisions and may be responsible for payment for, and quality of, the works contractors' works in the same way that a main contractor is responsible for the payment for, and quality of, a domestic sub-contractor's works in a traditional form of contract. The position will depend on the precise terms of the letters of intent.

There are no hard and fast rules on rights and obligations under a letter of intent but it may sometimes be possible to imply into the letters of intent contractual terms which reflect those contained in the management contract and works contracts. The extent to which a court will imply such terms will largely depend upon whether there is any certainty as to what the material terms of the contract would be. In *British Steel Corporation v Cleveland Bridge & Engineering Co Ltd* (1982) the court stated that the letter of intent in question did not amount to a 'contract' as it was impossible to say with any degree of certainty what the material terms of the contract would be because there were substantial areas which were still the subject of negotiations.

When the management contract and works contract are eventually entered into, following letters of intent, it appears that the terms of the contracts will govern the rights and obligations of the parties during the period covered by the letters of intent. In *Trollope & Colls Ltd v Atomic Power Constructions Ltd* (1963), the court implied in a contract a provision that its terms were to be retrospective and covered work previously done. This was on the basis that the term was necessary for the business efficacy of the contract.

It is therefore important for the parties to consider their respective rights and obligations if work is to proceed on the basis of letters of intent. It will often be prudent for a management contractor to ensure that any letter of intent from the employer affords him a suitable degree of protection before he instructs the works contractors to commence their respective packages.

2 DEFAULTING WORKS CONTRACTOR'S LIABILITY FOR LOSS AND EXPENSE

If a works contractor breaches his contract by failing to complete the works in the contractual period of completion (including any revised period), he will be liable to the management contractor for any direct loss and expense arising from this failure. Such loss and expense will include any liquidated damages which the management contractor is obliged to pay to the employer as a consequence of the works contractor's default.

It is important to recognise that the works contractor's failure to complete will not necessarily give rise to an extension of time under the management contract. However, it will give rise to an extension of time under their works contracts for other works contractors who are delayed by the works contractor in default (see for example Clause 2.10.7.1 of JCT Works Contract/2). In these circumstances, the project time may be exceeded without the management contractor having a right to an extension of time. This exposes him to the risk of paying liquidated damages to the employer under the management contract. The management contractor will therefore seek to recover from the defaulting works contractor the loss and expense incurred by other works contractors and his own loss and expense for his extended time and costs on site including any liquidated damages that he may be liable to pay to the employer. The management contractor will have the right to set off this loss and expense against money due under the works contract (including any retention monies held), notwithstanding the fiduciary obligation of the management contractor.

The relief provision

The management contractor may be entitled to rely on the relief provision for reimbursement of any shortfall in recovery from the works contractor in default. For example, if the defaulting works contractor goes into liquidation with the management contractor having made only a partial recovery, the employer will be required under the relief provision to make up the shortfall to the proper value of the claims of the works contractors who have incurred loss and expense. If, on the other hand, the management contractor pursues a solvent defaulting works contractor through arbitration or litigation, the employer will be required to fund the legal costs and will only be entitled to claim reimbursement from the management contractor to the extent that he successfully recovers legal costs from the works contractor in default.

Where a management contractor is liable to the employer for liquidated damages, he must include the amount of those liquidated damages as one head of his claim against the works contractor in default. The employer is not entitled to recover those liquidated damages from the management contractor, but must instead keep an account of the liquidated damages which he is entitled to recover from the management contractor. To the extent that the management contractor recovers those damages from the works contractor in default, he must pay over such sums to the employer. Any losses caused by the management contractor's own breaches or negligence must be borne by the management contractor and will not be reimbursed by the employer.

The relief provision may enable the works contractor to argue that the management contractor has suffered no loss and that consequently the management contractor cannot recover any losses from the works contractor. Because of this, JCT Works Contract/2 includes a provision that the works contractor will not contend that the management contractor has suffered or incurred no damage, loss or expense or that his liability to the management contractor should be reduced or extinguished by reason of the relief clause (Clause 1.6.2). This is discussed further in Chapter 11.

A difficulty that may arise in practice is that the management contractor may not recover enough from a defaulting works contractor to cover both the employer's liquidated damages and the management contractor's own loss and expense. The relief provision in management contracts does not usually provide for the employer to underwrite the management contractor's own loss and expense but only the loss and expense incurred by the works contractors not in default. Consideration must therefore be given to whether any recovery is to be apportioned between the employer and the management contractor. The JCT Management Contract does not deal with this difficulty. One solution to this potential problem is to provide that any sums recovered should be shared pro rata as between liquidated damages for the employer and loss and expense for the management contractor.

3 WORKS CONTRACTOR'S RIGHTS AGAINST MANAGEMENT CONTRACTOR

Extensions of time and reimbursement of loss and expense

The works contractor's contractual right to claim reimbursement of loss and expense caused to him by the events stipulated in the contract is separate from his common law rights to recover damages for breach of contract.

His contractual right to claim loss and expense is also independent of any entitlement to an extension of time. Under JCT Works Contract/2, for example, the works contractor is entitled to claim loss and expense if he can show a causal connection between the loss and expense and any of the matters set out in Clause 4.46, regardless of whether the loss and expense are time-related. Events giving rise to a claim for loss and expense are normally acts or defaults of the employer or his agents and might include, for example, the issue of late instructions, discrepancies in the contract documents, and failure to grant access and variations.

An important aspect of the management contractor's role is the duty to co-ordinate the performance of the various works contract packages. Any failure to do so may result in works contractors claiming extensions of time and loss and expense. The management contractor may have to bear such claims himself if they arise from his own breaches or negligence. His obligations will therefore involve careful planning and programming of the works.

If the progress of a works contractor's package is materially affected by the default of the management contractor, the works contractor will be entitled to recover his direct loss or expense from the management contractor. This will include any loss or expense caused by parties for whom the management contractor is responsible (including other works contractors).

Under Clause 3.22 of the JCT Management Contract, if a works contractor alleges a breach of the works contract by the management contractor, the management contractor must inform the architect and seek instructions, which may either involve settling the claim or defending the claim in arbitration or litigation. The clause provides that the employer shall reimburse the management contractor for amounts incurred in settling or defending the claim, as long as the obligation to pay such amounts does not arise from any breach of contract or negligence of the management contractor in discharging his obligations.

In practice, the management contractor will inform the architect of any such claim and will seek his instructions. The management contractor will particularly want to know whether the architect thinks the claim is due to the management contractor's own defaults and what proportion of the claim, if any, the employer will reimburse. He will need to establish the employer's position in clear terms before settling any claims. If he will receive no reimbursement from the employer, he will have to consider whether the claim has arisen out of the conduct of any defaulting works contractor whom he must pursue.

The management contractor will usually collaborate with the architect and quantity surveyor in the assessment of the works contractor's loss and expense. Under the JCT Management Contract, for example, any application for loss and expense must be passed on to the architect (together with the management contractor's observations).

Design obligations

As we have already indicated in Chapter 6, under the JCT Management Contract, the management contractor is required, during the pre-construction period, to advise on the practical implications of the professional team's drawings and specifications and to monitor, during construction, the progress of the design work and working drawings of all works contractors. He therefore has a (limited) involvement in design carried out by both the professional team and the works contractor.

Under JCT Works Contract/2, there is no obligation on the works contractor to produce design information so as not to delay the project. A situation can arise where the works contractor is late in producing the drawings he is required to provide for the professional team. This causes the architect to be late in issuing information to the management contractor, who is in turn late in issuing it to the works contractor. The works contractor is, however, not in default. This gives rise to an extension of time and an entitlement to loss and expense under the management contract and the works contract, even though those delays were caused by a delay by the works contractor. In these circumstances, the employer's only remedy is to pursue the works contractor under the terms of the standard form of employer/works contractor agreement without involving the management contractor.

The works contractor's responsibility for design is an area of weakness in the JCT Management Contract, which gives the management contractor insufficient control over the works contractor's design work. The employer may wish to give the management contractor extra powers – to co-ordinate the design or even to have some influence on its content. If the management contractor's responsibilities are to be extended in this way, it is necessary to consider carefully the nature of the management services to be provided by the management contractor. If one is dealing with the JCT Management Contract, this may involve significant amendments to the list of management services contained in the Third Schedule.

Interim certificates

The management contractor will usually have an obligation to transmit to the architect any requests made by the works contractor for information relating to the amounts included for him in interim certificates. The works contractor will have the right to be informed directly by the architect of the amount included for him in each relevant interim certificate (see JCT Management Contract Clause 8.3).

Practical completion

The management contractor will usually have an obligation to transmit to the architect any notification of practical completion by any works contractor and to convey his observations in writing on that notification to both the architect and the works contractor. The architect's consent is usually a precondition to the management contractor issuing a valid certificate of practical completion under the works contract (see JCT Management Contract Clause 8.3).

Extensions of time

The management contractor may be obliged to pass down to the works contractor any comments made by the architect on the extensions of time granted by the management contractor to the works contractor. In the JCT Management Contract, for example, the management contractor is only obliged to inform the works contractor if the architect dissents from the proposed extension of time. The management contractor is not usually obliged to inform the works contractor of the extensions of time awarded under the management contract.

CHAPTER 13

DISPUTE RESOLUTION

1 LITIGATION AND ARBITRATION

The court's powers

The extent of the court's powers to resolve construction and engineering disputes was highlighted by the decision in *Northern Regional Health Authority v Derek Crouch Construction Co Ltd* (1984). In this case, the Court of Appeal held that where a construction contract contains an arbitration clause empowering the arbitrator to review certificates and decisions of the architect, and a dispute arising under that contract is referred to litigation instead of arbitration, the court will not be able to exercise the wide powers conferred on the arbitrator by the arbitration clause.

Since the architect's decisions are often in issue in construction contracts, the *Crouch* decision considerably reduces the scope for taking such disputes to court. However, the problems created by *Crouch* are in limited circumstances alleviated by Section 100 of the Courts and Legal Services Act 1990, which amends Section 43 of the Supreme Court Act 1981. This amendment enables the High Court to exercise the powers of the arbitrator as set out in the contract, provided that all parties to the arbitration agreement agree. By the very nature of a dispute, though, such agreement may not be forthcoming. (It is important to note that s 100 only applies to contracts which contain an arbitration agreement and not to contracts which contain clauses conferring jurisdiction on the courts.)

In practice, *Crouch* will usually work to the detriment of the contractor who, more often than not, is the party seeking to review a certificate or decision. In such circumstances, the limitation on the court's powers to review such certificates and decisions will be of little concern to the employer. It is not uncommon for employers to be willing to accept the limitations on the court's powers. They are usually prepared to accept the certificates or decisions of an architect whom they have appointed and in whose ability, judgment and independence they have confidence.

Multipartite proceedings

In construction management contracts, where the employer enters into a number of trade contracts direct with the trade contractors, there is a risk of multipartite proceedings. The courts are an appropriate forum for the resolution of such disputes, since they have a number of procedural rules to accommodate multipartite proceedings. Construction management contracts therefore usually provide for litigation as the form of dispute resolution. In order to overcome the difficulties caused by *Crouch*, such contracts usually provide that the parties agree to confer jurisdiction on the courts to 'open up, review and revise' certificates.

The point has not yet been tested in the courts, but it seems that the courts cannot be bound to accept such jurisdiction and there is no certainty that they will always be willing to do so. Although it is difficult to predict how the courts will react in circumstances where the parties agree to confer jurisdiction, the case of *Othieno v Mr & Mrs Cooper* (1991) suggests that there may be a tendency for the courts to shy away from accepting it.

One problem with arbitration which arises frequently in construction and engineering disputes is that there are often more than two parties involved who have not entered into arbitration agreements with each other. This may lead to the significant costs of more than one arbitration hearing and the possibility of conflicting arbitral awards based on different findings of fact. A number of procedural rules are available in the courts to resolve the position of all the parties in one hearing, thus avoiding these difficulties.

Joinder of arbitration clauses

This problem may to some extent be overcome by the incorporation of a joinder clause providing for multipartite arbitration. Although joinder clauses are often found in traditional contracts, they are particularly important in management contracts because any dispute arising between the employer and management contractor is most likely to relate to the works or works contractors. It would be unsatisfactory for such disputes to be dealt with in two separate arbitrations under the management contract and under the works contract.

A joinder of arbitration clause will usually provide that if a dispute or difference under the management contract is referred to arbitration and raises issues which are substantially the same as or are connected with issues raised in a related dispute already referred to arbitration, then the new arbitration must be joined with the related dispute arbitration. The related dispute is usually one between the employer and the works contractor (if such a contract has been entered into), or between the management contractor and any works contractor, or between a works contractor and any nominated supplier.

Whether any dispute can be said to be 'substantially the same as or connected with issues raised in a related dispute' will be a matter of fact in each case. In *Higgs & Hill Building Ltd v Campbell Denis Ltd* (1982), the court had to consider who should determine whether 'the dispute or difference to be referred to arbitration under the sub-contract raises issues which are substantially the same as or connected with issues raised in a related dispute'. In this case the related dispute was between the employer and the contractor under the main contract. This was held to be a matter for the judgment of the main contractor, who, as a party to both the main contract and the subcontract, was best placed to make the judgment. However, in *Hyundai Engineering v Active Building* (1988), the court held that this question was not for the contractor but should be determined by the court. We believe that this decision is to be preferred, on the basis that one party to a prospective arbitration cannot unilaterally determine whether the necessary conditions are fulfilled.

2 THE ROLE OF THE MANAGEMENT CONTRACTOR

Unlike a construction manager in construction management contracts, a management contractor has two distinct roles which can be difficult to reconcile, particularly when dealing with the consideration of extensions of time under the works contracts. On the one hand the management contractor is required to collaborate with the professional team. On the other, he will find himself protecting his own position and that of the works contractor. Occasions will arise, for example, when the management contractor seeks an extension of time because the works contractor is entitled to an extension of time after late receipt of drawings or instructions. In this respect, the management contractor is in the same position as the main contractor would be in a traditional form of contract.

One of the essential differences between a traditional contract and a management contract is that under the works contract the management contractor decides what extension of time, if any, is to be given to the works contractor. The management contractor will not usually be obliged to consult the architect other than to notify him of his decision to grant an extension of time. The management contractor will probably not be bound by the architect's opinion on the matter and he will be free to exercise his independent judgment, unlike the main contractor under JCT 80 who requires the architect's consent to award an extension of time.

The management contractor's role in dealing with applications for extensions of time is a central part of the management of the project. It is important that he keeps the professional team informed of his decisions as such information is necessary to monitor the progress of costs to the project and often gives rise to a corresponding extension of time under the management contract. It is not unreasonable that the management contractor is required to exercise the disciplines required of an architect under a traditional form of contract as one of his primary skills on the project will be his ability to programme and control the works.

One of the difficulties that may arise as a result of the divided responsibility for awarding extensions of time is that the management contractor may award the works contractor a longer extension of time than he obtains from the architect under the management contract. If this happens, the management contractor may be liable to pay liquidated damages to the employer without being able to recover them from the works contractor. This risk highlights the importance of notifying the architect of any extensions of time that the management contractor is proposing to award to the works contractor.

In construction management contracts, though, the construction manager exercises the role of the architect under a traditional form of contract but will not be concerned with his own liability for liquidated damages.

3 ADJUDICATION

Adjudication as a form of intermediate dispute resolution is becoming increasingly common in construction and engineering contracts. The JCT Management Contract makes no provision for any form of intermediate dispute resolution. However, the adjudication procedure is used to a limited extent to resolve any dispute between a works contractor and the management contractor over the amount the management contractor intends to set off.

In contrast with arbitration, adjudication generally consists of a procedure whereby an adjudicator (whose identity is normally agreed in the contract) will arrive at a decision on a dispute or difference. The adjudicator's decision is final and binding (unless it is referred to arbitration within a stipulated period) and is implemented immediately. The procedure leading up to the adjudicator's decision will vary from case to case but will not usually be as lengthy as arbitration or court proceedings.

Adjudication as a form of intermediate dispute resolution is most appropriate in long-running contracts where the parties require a swift decision which immediately determines their rights and obligations, subject to a right (which must be exercised within a stipulated period) to arbitrate the adjudicator's decision following the completion of the contract. In practice, the parties will often accept the adjudicator's decision and will not proceed to arbitration. In such cases, the adjudication procedure has the significant advantage of resolving disputes speedily and cheaply. An adjudicator's decision is sometimes viewed by the parties as an indication of the most probable decision that an arbitral tribunal will reach and in these circumstances, the parties may be reluctant to proceed to arbitration. But in complex disputes where large sums are at stake, arbitration is more likely to follow the adjudication procedure as the parties are more likely to want a further opportunity to present their case more fully and comprehensively. In these circumstances, the adjudication procedure may still help to reduce the areas of dispute which are to be referred to arbitration.

It is important to remember that the Arbitration Acts will not apply to an adjudicator. Consequently, the parties may have to resort to the courts to enforce any decision reached by the adjudicator. In *A Cameron Ltd v John Mowlem & Co Plc* (1991), the Court of Appeal held that an adjudicator's decision under Clause 24 of JCT DOM/1 was not enforceable as an arbitral award as an adjudicator's decision has an 'ephemeral and subordinate character' which makes it impossible for the decision to be described as an award or an arbitration agreement.

CHAPTER 14

RISK ALLOCATION

1 HARD AND SOFT MANAGEMENT CONTRACTS

The preceding chapters have illustrated a number of ways in which management contracting systems seek to distribute various risks between the principal parties. They have also shown that the main intention of management contracting is to place a relatively low risk on the management contractor himself. This is achieved principally through the operation of the relief provision.

Although the JCT 87 standard form of management contract now provides a baseline, other forms of management contract are in use and the JCT form itself is often amended. Such forms and amendments may alter the balance of risk between employer and management contractor in a number of areas. It is beyond the scope of this chapter to explore the theoretical effect that adjustment has on the advantages or disadvantages of the system, but examples of some common types of variant may be noted. Contracts where the balance of risk is shifted significantly towards the management contractor, equating his position more to that of a traditional main contractor, are sometimes referred to as 'hard' management contracts. 'Soft' contracts are those where the management contractor's risk is relatively diminished.

Variants as to cost

The definition of prime cost may be varied. Prime cost may include or exclude certain specific items (such as particular kinds of site office overheads) or certain general descriptions of cost (for example, additional costs incurred through the alleged negligence of the management contractor).

Hard contracts may include mechanisms for fixing various elements of the cost as lump sums. This approach is frequently adopted to cover some or all of the management contractor's preliminaries. The JCT Management Contract allows the employer to require a lump sum in lieu of prime cost and provides for an unspecified 'memorandum' to be included, stating how that agreed initial lump sum is to be adjusted as a result of 'compliance by the management contractor with instructions'. Fixed sums may also apply to management staff rates and operative rates.

Hard contracts may place an upper limit on part or all of the prime cost. A guaranteed maximum price may apply, based on either initial cost estimates or some sort of budgetary adjustment mechanism which takes into account limited cost variation factors (such as the kind of fluctuations seen under a traditional main contract).

The management fee may be calculated and subject to adjustment in a multiplicity of ways. It may be expressed as a fixed sum or as a percentage rate to be applied to the final prime cost. If it is a fixed sum, it may be adjustable to reflect increases or decreases of the final prime cost outside certain tolerances of the initial estimated prime cost. The JCT Management Contract adopts this approach with a norm of a 5% tolerance.

Further mechanisms for adjusting the fee may be introduced in order to provide incentives for the management contractor to achieve cost or time targets. This process requires the calculation of a target cost and the creation of a mechanism for adjusting this by reference to specified variation factors (see Chapter 9, Section 4).

Finally, just as the prime cost may be capped or limited, so a hard contract may introduce a mechanism for limiting or gearing the management fee in line with limits on the prime cost.

Variants as to time

A management contract commonly incorporates a break clause giving the employer the option of dispensing with the services of the management contractor at the end of the pre-construction period. It will not always be to the employer's advantage to include such a provision, since the consequences and cost of operating it may outweigh any gains to be derived from continuing the project with a new contractor (assuming that the employer wishes to continue with the project at all). The contract may therefore be softened by omitting the break procedure. The resultant reduction in uncertainty for the management contractor should have some impact on the size of the management fee. However, the employer will normally wish to retain rights of termination for particular events.

Another consideration is the extent to which some works contractors' packages (typically for goods and materials that have a long ordering lead time) need to be let during the pre-construction period, well before construction begins. If the management contractor can let advance works packages, the effect of the break clause may be somewhat illusory unless provision is made for the assignment of those works packages either to the employer or to a substitute management contractor.

The management contractor's liability for liquidated damages for delay may be linked to his ability to recover liquidated damages from works contractors in default. Changes in the degree to which (or circumstances in which) the management contractor is held liable for liquidated damages provide a major means for adjusting the balance of risk between employer and management contractor.

A hard management contract may leave the management contractor liable for liquidated damages irrespective of whether he can recover his costs from defaulting works contractors. A middle road would be for the management contractor to be relieved from liability for liquidated damages unless he can recover the appropriate sum from defaulting works contractors to the extent that he can properly attribute to them responsibility for the delay. A soft approach would be for the management contractor to be absolved of all liability for delay other than the requirement to account for liquidated damages recovered from works contractors, except where the employer can show that failure was on the part of the management contractor rather than a works contractor.

Variants as to quality or performance

Although the management contractor usually undertakes purely management services, with all construction works being included in works contract packages, there are many situations in which the management contractor himself or, perhaps more frequently, an associated company within the management contractor's group, wishes to tender for a part of the works. This is often the case for the provision of site services (such as cleaning and clearance) and the provision of attendances and facilities for works contractors.

If the management contractor himself becomes directly responsible for particular works or services of this nature there will be no scope for the operation of a relief clause as to his liability for such services. This will obviously harden the contract.

The same principle may be applied where such works or services are to be provided by an associated company of the management contractor. Where this happens, the relief principle may be inapplicable and the management contractor may be required, in effect, to take the risk of his associated company performing inadequately or becoming insolvent.

The most likely means of altering the balance of risk between employer and management contractor in the area of performance or quality of work is through the different ways of expressing the relief clause itself, since the relief clause is the principal mechanism for setting the balance of risk in the first place.

A soft approach would be a clause specifically exempting the management contractor from all liability for works contractors, effectively framed to give the employer the onus of showing that a defect in performance has been caused by the management contractor rather than by a works contractor's breach. A compromise would be for the clause to exempt the management contractor from liability while leaving on the management contractor the burden of attributing the cause of a problem to a works contractor's breach rather than his own performance of his services. A hard approach would be to frame the relief clause so as to cover only inability of the management contractor to recover from works contractors due to their insolvency. A rock-hard approach would be to dispense with the relief clause altogether, as does the First Edition of the ICE's New Engineering Contract (see Chapter 11, Section 1). This may be thought to negate completely the intended low-risk nature of the contract for the management contractor.

2 THE READING AND SOUTHAMPTON REPORTS

Two reports, published in 1991 and based on wide-ranging research in the industry, explore in some detail the nature and relative merits of management contracting and construction management as systems of construction procurement. *Construction Management Forum - Report and Guidance* is published by the Centre for Strategic Studies in Construction, University of Reading. *Roles, Responsibilities and Risks in Management Contracting*, by B Curtis, S Ward and C Chapman, was published as CIRIA Special Publication 81 and is generally referred to as the Southampton Report. This chapter concludes with a brief summary and comparison of their findings.

The Reading Report

The Reading Report concludes, in essence, that employers inclined to adopt a management system for construction procurement should prefer construction management to management contracting as the system most calculated to realise their goals. Key points stated as leading to this conclusion (as explained in Part IV of the Report, comprising the reports of the working parties of the forum) are as follows.

Transparency

Construction management reflects the true relationship between the parties more accurately than management contracting, which to an extent disguises the level of risk borne by the employer by giving the management contractor the appearance of a traditional main contractor.

Simplicity

Construction management reflects the basic nature of the relationship between manager and employer in providing a service for a fee. A management contract, however, goes through the complicated procedure of placing the construction risk on the manager so that he can engage the works contractors, only then to remove the risk through the operation of the relief clause.

Cost control

The construction manager is considered to be more closely identified than the management contractor with the establishment and subsequent development of the cost plan, the critical document for cost control of the project.

Enforceability

In construction management, because the employer contracts directly with the works contractor, there are none of the problems which may be caused by the relief principle and attendant 'no loss' difficulties if the management contractor has to enforce works contracts.

Balance

A construction manager's basis for appointment is very similar in nature to that of the designer. He is clearly in a relationship of consultancy with the employer. The Report suggests that this makes it easier for the construction manager to be appointed at the same time as the designer – in contrast with a management contractor who may not be appointed early enough to make a useful initial contribution to the design and definition of other aspects of the project.

Participation

Construction management enables, indeed requires, the employer to maintain close involvement in the running of the project in order to make day to day decisions, pay works contractors and so on. With a management contractor in place, the employer remains at one remove from the works contractors and the day to day carrying out of the project. The employer needs to recognise the additional direct involvement (including, amongst other things, management time) that construction management will entail for him.

Payment

The Reading Report suggests that evidence shows that works contractors may be paid more quickly in a construction management system, since it dispenses with one link in the payment chain (the intermediate main or management contractor). The Report says that this may result in lower-priced tenders from works contractors.

Flexibility

In construction management, the terms of the different works contracts can be altered to suit varying circumstances, whereas under a management contract it is assumed that all works contracts let by the management contractor will be in the same form, so as to fit into the overall structure.

Termination

The Reading Report suggests that it is easier for the employer to terminate a construction management agreement than a management contract because of the procedural difficulty in the latter case of having to assign or novate all the management contractor's works contracts to a new management contractor.

Professional roles

In construction management, the designer works alongside the construction manager, with the latter usually being responsible for issuing instructions to works contractors. Under a management contract, the designer usually retains the traditional role of supervising officer, issuing instructions to the management contractor who then has to pass them on to the works contractors. The quantity surveyor's role may be reduced in construction management because the construction manager is likely to issue certificates based on his own valuations and there is no main contract under which valuations have to be made or certificates issued. This effectively gives the construction manager both power and responsibility for cost control, in contrast with a management contract where the quantity surveyor may retain the power (through making valuations for certificates) but the management contractor has the responsibility to control works contractors' costs.

The emphatic conclusion and recommendation of the Reading Report is that construction management is to be preferred as a system for all of the above reasons.

The Southampton Report

The Southampton Report, however, concludes that there is no universally applicable precept for determining which system will be preferable in all conceivable circumstances. The Report evaluates the advantages and disadvantages of management systems in general, but does not consider them to point conclusively to either construction management or management contracting as the better system of the two.

The Southampton Report concentrates on the consequences for the employer of managing risks in particular ways. Its central argument is that the employer should undertake his own risk analysis in individual cases, determine how he wishes risk to be apportioned between the parties, and choose the contracting system - management contracting, construction management or a variant of either - which best suits that risk analysis.

Ultimately, therefore, the Southampton Report considers that the employer's own resources and wishes, the abilities of available works contractors and the nature of the project as a whole will dictate which system is preferable in particular instances. Finally, while apparently supporting some but not all of the Reading Report points, the Southampton Report concludes that these points do not add up overall to a case for construction management over management contracting.